Praise for _Th_

Business is there for the long term, not the short term. It doesn't need leadership; it needs _great_ leadership. It also needs a balance of success and sustainability and that is what this book is all about. SINCLAIR BEECHAM, FOUNDER, PRET A MANGER

Now more than ever the world needs leaders who can lead businesses without limits. We don't need leaders who just follow the crowd locked in groupthink. _The Infinite leader_ shows that type of real leadership needed on the rocky road ahead. EDMUND V KING OBE, PRESIDENT, AA

Leadership is dynamic and complex. What worked in the past will not work now. This is true across every sector of society, and a failure of leadership ultimately destroys hope and a belief in the future. This wonderful new book provides a beacon to guide our path, defining the attitudes and principles needed by our leaders to build a better society. My warmest congratulations to Chris Lewis and Pippa Malmgren. PROFESSOR RUSSELL FOSTER CBE, FRS, DIRECTOR OF THE SLEEP AND CIRCADIAN NEUROSCIENCE INSTITUTE, UNIVERSITY OF OXFORD

By taking us on a journey, challenging our perceptions, inspiring thought and stimulating new ideas, Chris Lewis and Pippa Malmgren practise what they preach in _The Infinite Leader_. THE RT HON GREG CLARK MP

Prescient and pragmatic in equal measure, _The Infinite Leader_ could just become the bible for post-COVID-19 leadership. ALISON CORK, ENTREPRENEUR

As an educator, the limits of traditional busiess school approaches to leadership are uncomfortably exposed in the opening pages of *The Infinite Leader*. The authors' thesis is persuasive: 21st-century leadership must navigate complexity and ambiguity as never before and requires a capacity for 'situational fluency' to underpin and motivate our actions. To help us achieve this, Chris Lewis and Pippa Malmgren offer a powerful model of leadership that brings the rational, spiritual, emotional and physical elements in our thinking and feeling into balance. Well researched and highly accessible, this fully deserves an 'essential read' label on its cover. PROFESSOR DAVID BROWN, LANCASTER UNIVERSITY MANAGEMENT SCHOOL

This is a *very* timely book. As companies, organizations and work itself are reinventing themselves, *The Infinite Leader* provides original and thought-provoking insight into how leaders can harness the collective intelligence of their teams to successfully navigate uncertainty as well as new and ever-changing circumstances. Chris Lewis and Pippa Malmgren are brilliant in their guidance to manage the imbalances, foster deeper inclusion and ensure greater integrity. HELEN ALDERSON, INTERNATIONAL COMMITTEE OF THE RED CROSS (ICRC)

The Infinite Leader comes out at a critical time when the loss and anxieties created by a global pandemic and the clamour for change with movements such as Black Lives Matter highlight the need for a leadership which we all have a responsibility to bring. This book will help the reader shine a spotlight on the elements of good leadership while highlighting the ways that leadership has become too focused, short term, tactical and self-interested. It provides insights into the important balance between legacy and vision, a leadership to build trust and unity rather than to drive us apart. CHARLOTTE LINDSEY CURTET, MANAGEMENT CONSULTANT

This book is about everything that we knew and could not articulate ourselves. And what we did not know and was not explained to us. MILENKO PRVAČKI, SENIOR FELLOW, LASALLE COLLEGE OF ARTS

Timing is everything with success, and what better time to release *The Infinite Leader* to educate and enthuse the leadership ability we all possess. This book captures the complex balancing act leaders will face moving forward as our sense of normality is confronted by a more demanding 'urbane' human, outmoded industry systems, an accelerated 'beyond GDP' movement, disrupted economies and societies and pressured natural environment. The mental and physical balancing act required will be no mean feat, and this book is an ideal companion on this expedition. TOM SAVIGAR, FOUNDER, AVANSERE AS; CO-OWNER, THE FUTURE LABORATORY

Capital is the most powerful force for evil on the planet. This book talks about the balance needed for capitalism to survive. BILL THORNHILL, EDITOR, GLOBALCAPITAL

The Infinite Leader is another tour de force from Chris Lewis and Pippa Malmgren and comes along at a propitious moment in our time. Their work reminds us that strong leaders are grown, not born, and before we can inspire those around us, we must first take a hard look at ourselves. As a leader in business, I'm incorporating many of Chris and Pippa's insights from this book to my entire leadership team! KENNETH TODOROV, BRIG GEN, USAF (RET), VICE PRESIDENT AND GENERAL MANAGER, NORTHROP GRUMMAN DEFENSE SYSTEMS

Entrepreneurs of all kinds can find freedom in their mission but they can also lose it in the process. This book provides resources to re-ground and refresh that sense of freedom to support and raise up a generation of leaders that can sustain a 'whole' team and a spirit of invention and impact.

Unlocking insights that draw on practical ethics, aspects of anthropology and deep experience of founding and renewing real organizations, *The Infinite Leader* is a resource for all those leading in shape-shifting times.

The call to leadership is as old as humanity but new environments need us to refashion what has been, and repurpose what is to come. This book is a resource for renewal for all those responsible for that vocation from the private equity backed innovator to the coalface community organizer to the top team of a major health system.

From cardinals to health managers to community organizers, the context, nature and potential impact of leadership is changing with sometimes confusing road stops along the journey. This book is a brilliant resource for leaders who want to refresh their own spirit and unlock the full range of talents, insights and energy that their teams and allies bring to that new challenge. FRANCIS DAVIS FRGS, PROFESSOR OF RELIGION, COMMUNITIES AND PUBLIC POLICY, UNIVERSITY OF BIRMINGHAM, UK; FELLOW, HELEN SUZMAN FOUNDATION, SOUTH AFRICA; PROFESSORIAL FELLOW, UNIVERSITY OF OXFORD; ADVISER TO INTERNATIONAL NON-PROFITS AND AN AWARD-WINNING SOCIAL ENTREPRENEUR

The Infinite Leader challenges by raising key questions and exploring potential answers but allowing readers to come to their own conclusions in a world where values in global business are often seen as not only different but often irreconcilable. LORD CHADLINGTON, ENTREPRENEUR

Thoughtful and provoking. An important, prescient and well-presented inquiry on the critical values and skills needed for leadership in today's morally bankrupt world. Chris Lewis and Pippa Malmgren challenge us to engage, at the crossroads of multiple crises, to do a better job with selecting our leaders. WES PAUL, FOUNDER AND EXECUTIVE CHAIRMAN, GEMIN-I ANALYTICS LTD

The Infinite Leader takes a penetrating look at the incredible complexity of leadership within a truly contemporary and brutally honest context. Yet, neither does it soften the truth – that leadership and entrepreneurship is still a tough, relentless and personal journey. Importantly, the subtle and diverse values of the team in the context of leadership is probed skilfully – turning out some uncomfortable truths. A thoughtful and necessary read, with nuanced argument in every page. SIR GEORGE ZAMBELLAS, ENTREPRENEUR, INVESTOR, LEADER IN TECHNOLOGY, AND FORMER FIRST SEA LORD

Chris Lewis and Pippa Malmgren always provide unique and relevant perspectives on the key leadership issues and trends of the day. This book is no exception. I highly recommend it. ROBERT J HERBOLD, FORMER CHIEF OPERATING OFFICER, MICROSOFT CORPORATION

The Infinite Leader is a must-read for anyone in a leadership role; that's everyone. The latest Chris Lewis and Pippa Malmgren collaboration has produced a wonderfully thoughtful and thought-provoking piece, offering insights aplenty, opening us to reflection and contemplation throughout.

At a time of great uncertainty, *The Infinite Leader* homes in on the universal truth: not only are we all leaders, we all need, more than ever, to lead. At a time of instant communication, or often, what passes as such, we are afforded the time to pause, to ponder, crucially, to take the time to think. LORD HOLMES OF RICHMOND, PARALYMPIAN

Achieving the right balance between short-term and long-term interests is perplexing for many leaders. *The Infinite Leader* offers a wise, insightful, thought-provoking way forward for 21st-century leaders. Chris Lewis and Pippa Malmgren offer a new appreciation for the necessity of balance and moral purpose based on a fairer, more inclusive, human-centred approach to leadership and team building. They urge leaders to reflect, renew and reset the balance – it starts from within.

In this way, the book moves to identify the kind of leadership needed at the helms of our modern businesses. Their insightful solutions are not the product of armchair contemplation but have emerged from the sweat and tears of actual business delivery and growth efforts. Their work on leadership is therefore powerful not just because it is evidence-based but because it is practical. They succeed in going far beyond the rhetoric of moral purpose to lay out in stark terms what is the real leadership reform agenda.

Readers accustomed to insightfulness and breadth on leadership will not be disappointed by *The Infinite Leader*. Those discovering the authors for the first time will be profoundly impressed. *The Infinite Leader* gives leaders and entrepreneurs a unique insight into a more healthy, sustainable approach to delivering and growing their businesses for positive socio-economic impact. *The Infinite Leader* therefore offers an essential perspective on the kind of leadership needed in these turbulent times. AMIR HUSSAIN, COE (CHIEF OF EVERYTHING), YEME ARCHITECTS

Chris Lewis and Pippa Malmgren have done it again! This powerful, accessible, optimistic vision exceeds expectations and gets to the heart of what is balanced living leadership and culture creation. More challengingly, it explores how can we meaningfully assess leadership performance with a relevant and ethical dynamic model.

In a world with radically new emerging priorities and practices, it engagingly explores why we need to study the very best balanced leaders who listen, love, build and embed co-constructed collaborative cultures to earn the confidences given from their teams.

Never in our lifetimes have we more needed less greed and short-termism driven by reckless over-confidence, because leadership affects everything. Every business, educational and health institution, every community, team and individual... because we are all leaders.

Enjoy this powerful, optimistic and inspiring vision. It really can greatly influence and change your thinking, improve performance and be helpful, and is also a great, fun read. Treat yourself. You are really worth it! STEVE FRAMPTON, PRESIDENT, ASSOCIATION OF COLLEGES

Having spent the last 35 years leading projects in some of the most challenging communities in Britain, I know firsthand the truth that is in this book: that real and effective leadership has to be earned and is given as a gift by others. It can never be assumed. Once it is, you're lost. A lesson many of our politicians would do well to learn. What you say, how you act and what you do have to stack up. Forget the illusion of the separation of the private and public role. They are connected; you are one person. This book takes us very helpfully into this moral territory, which is all about who you are and what you do. Chris Lewis and Pippa Malmgren have once again pointed us, amid all the noise and confusion of our age, to some important historical and practical truths that are always true, everywhere and for all peoples. We all have more in common than we realize, and this book reminds us of our shared humanity. LORD MAWSON OBE, FOUNDER AND PRESIDENT, THE BROMLEY-BY-BOW CENTRE, EAST LONDON

Organizations need to deliver in the face of changing and increasing challenges, but what, for you, will be your personal response to the challenges presented by COVID-19, Black Lives Matter, deep recession, the rise of China?

Our world has changed fundamentally, and it has changed overnight. Such ambiguous and uncertain times require us to evolve fast, build smart partnerships and drive the recovery agenda hard. We will be well served to show up as the best version of ourselves, but what does that mean? For sure, embracing diversity really matters as groupthink exists to narrow our options and creates dangerous blind spots. And, importantly, if we are to become better than before, we probably need to look to creating a culture where innovation and ideas flourish.

These imperatives present significant organizational challenges for colleagues across the community but this collaboration between Chris Lewis and Pippa Malmgren presents a much-needed playbook at a moment when we are all facing the abyss. JACQUELINE DE ROJAS CBE, PRESIDENT, TECHUK

More so than any other time in the past 40 years, we are taking calls from the leaders of companies, in the wake of COVID-19, economic uncertainty and a new civil rights movement, saying: 'We want to do the right thing, but we don't know how.' It's not a lack of imagination, but instead challenges so deep and historical that they require Herculean efforts and the will to see them through. The always imaginative and thought-provoking Chris Lewis and Pippa Malmgren step into the void and offer solid advice that starts with the mirror. What can we do to be the change we want? As always, they deliver with Biblical-level insights, solid analytics and the soundest of advice. Indispensable. RICHARD LEVICK, CHAIRMAN AND CEO, LEVICK

The Infinite Leader is a powerful follow-up to *The Leadership Lab*. Pippa Malmgren and Chris Lewis convincingly convey that modern leadership incorporates all stakeholders and that a successful leader focuses on how things – and not only what things – are done.

This book will be *The Seven Effective Habits* and *On Becoming a Leader* for this generation of leaders. It should be required reading at all business schools and corporate boards!

Great cultures and missions succeed and endure. In *The Infinite Leader*, Pippa and Chris clearly articulate the qualities of leadership necessary to build an enduring enterprise and to effectively meet all stakeholder needs. GREG WILLIAMSON, HEAD OF STRATEGY, PLURIBUS LABS

Chris Lewis and Pippa Malmgren, that winning combination, are back in action setting the pace on what leaders need to do to succeed in the new normal. SIR ANTHONY SELDON MA, PHD, FRSA, MBA, FRHISS, VICE-CHANCELLOR OF THE UNIVERSITY OF BUCKINGHAM, CONTEMPORARY HISTORIAN, EDUCATIONALIST, COMMENTATOR AND POLITICAL AUTHOR

If you were to ask people what they think of our current political and business leaders, they would probably reply 'What leadership?' We are seeing two-dimensional leaders, not leaders with an infinite range of attitudes, behaviours and philosophies. This book addresses that deficit, and in an entertaining, innovative and 'off the wall' way. It is not just another leadership book; it is *the* infinitive leader's manual – don't miss it! PROFESSOR SIR CARY COOPER CBE, 50TH ANNIVERSARY PROFESSOR OF ORGANIZATIONAL PSYCHOLOGY AND HEALTH, ALLIANCE MANCHESTER BUSINESS SCHOOL, UNIVERSITY OF MANCHESTER

Perhaps the biggest challenge for any leader is to make any positive measurable social impact. PETER DE HAAN, CHAIRMAN, OPUS TRUST

For the last 20 years, many of us have fought a battle for more balanced leadership. This book explains why it's no longer just a matter of social justice. It's about economic efficiency and performance as well. BARONESS JENKIN OF KENNINGTON

Chris Lewis and Pippa Malmgren shine light upon what leadership ought to be and what it can be. Their insights are a rallying call that real leadership is not about changing others, rather it is about changing yourself. BRIGADIER GENERAL GARY KRAHN, USA (RET), HEAD, LA JOLLA COUNTRY DAY SCHOOL

The Infinite Leader is a wake-up call and could not be more timely. Challenging, insightful and inspiring, it unpacks the greatest challenges facing organizations today and provides a clarion call for leadership response. The central thesis of balance and agility across intersecting criteria is compelling, as is the call for greater love in leadership where its absence is costing us dearly. Our brighter future requires leaders to be weavers of the warp and weft of social fabric and to be daily champions of our values underpinned by a strong culture. This makes eminent sense to me. NICK CAPLIN CB, CHIEF EXECUTIVE OFFICER, BLIND VETERANS UK

The Infinite Leader strikes at some of the major challenges today globally, not only in business but also in government. The points on changes in social communications, economics, management of resources and divisions facing society help the reader understand what is required to be a true leader. *The Infinite Leader* shows us why leaders fail to understand how to be effective and transparent in building networks and true partnerships. The framework of the chapters brings the reader to a better understanding of the processes at work when leadership isn't there and how to better approach this subject with lessons learned through the authors' international corporate leadership experiences. THOMAS ZAMPIERI PHD, PRESIDENT, BLINDED VETERANS ASSOCIATION

If you look at the sky tonight you might see millions of stars. They are there, even if you cannot see them. *The Infinite Leader* challenges traditional thinking about leadership, promoting the concept of leadership balance to make us more creative, productive and effective as leaders. Up to the minute, I thoroughly recommend *The Infinite Leader* to all aspiring leaders. Read it, and you will see more stars. PETER PEREIRA GRAY, CHIEF EXECUTIVE OFFICER, INVESTMENT DIVISION, THE WELLCOME TRUST

Chris Lewis and Pippa Malmgren have once again seized on issues surrounding the leadership zeitgeist. Their thought leadership in these confused and disrupted times cuts to the core. *The Infinite Leader* positions thoughtful and valuable understanding in an articulate and digestible formula. This is a contemporary rule book, acting as a navigation tool, to help those looking for insight into the modern codes of leadership. MARK BORKOWSKI, FOUNDER, BORKOWSKI PR

The Infinite Leader

*Balancing the demands of
modern business leadership*

Chris Lewis and
Pippa Malmgren

Kogan Page
INSPIRE

First published in Great Britain and the United States in 2021 by Kogan Page Limited

2nd Floor, 45 Gee Street	122 W 27th St, 10th Floor	4737/23 Ansari Road
London	New York, NY 10001	Daryaganj
EC1V 3RS	USA	New Delhi 110002
United Kingdom		India

www.koganpage.com

Kogan Page books are printed on paper from sustainable forests.

ISBNs
Hardback	978 1 78966 651 9
Paperback	978 1 78966 649 6
Ebook	978 1 78966 650 2

British Library Cataloguing-in-Publication Data
A CIP record for this book is available from the British Library.

Library of Congress Cataloging-in-Publication Data
Names: Lewis, Chris, 1961- author. | Malmgren, Philippa, author.
Title: The infinite leader: balancing the demands of modern business leadership / Chris Lewis and Pippa Malmgren.
Description: 1st Edition. | New York: Kogan Page Ltd, 2020. | Includes bibliographical references and index.
Identifiers: LCCN 2020031489 (print) | LCCN 2020031490 (ebook) | ISBN 9781789666519 (hardback) | ISBN 9781789666496 (paperback) | ISBN 9781789666502 (ebook)
Subjects: LCSH: Leadership. | Communication in management.
Classification: LCC HD57.7 .L4757 2020 (print) | LCC HD57.7 (ebook) | DDC 658.4/092–dc23
LC record available at https://lccn.loc.gov/2020031489
LC ebook record available at https://lccn.loc.gov/2020031490

Typeset by Integra Software Services, Pondicherry
Print production managed by Jellyfish
Printed and bound by CPI Group (UK) Ltd, Croydon CR0 4YY

Contents

List of figures and tables

About the authors

Chris Lewis and Dr Pippa Malmgren are both entrepreneurs, consultants and authors. Their first collaboration was *The Leadership Lab: Understanding leadership in the 21st century*. This won Leadership Book of the Year and Business Book of the Year in 2019 in the UK, the 2019 New York City Business Big Book Award as well as the 2020 Independent Press Award, Leadership. Chris's *Too Fast to Think: How to reclaim your creativity in a hyper connected work culture* and Pippa's *Signals: How everyday signs can help us navigate the world's turbulent economy* also achieved bestseller status in the US and the UK.

Chris founded one of the world's largest marketing firms and advises a variety of CEOs, senior politicians, members of the royal family and international philanthropic organizations.

Pippa was Special Adviser to President George W Bush and advises CEOs, prime ministers, and the heads of major banks and the world's largest institutional investors. She also founded a robotics firm and speaks regularly at firms like Google and American Express and major banks.

Foreword

When I was a teenager at Cambridge Rindge and Latin School in Massachusetts, I won an essay contest on how to address racial tension. It was a difficult time. My community had just survived a racially motivated stabbing and local clergy were maintaining a presence in the hallways. The pride I felt when I saw my own rector, Reverend W Murray Kenney, walking the halls has stayed with me throughout my life. I remember reflecting, in the essay, that racial tensions were like a pendulum. The laws of physics required a period of imbalance on the other extreme as a necessary counterpoint. I believed that a 'social centre' would be achieved and that society would ultimately settle. Indeed, as evidenced by the continuing unrest in race, gender, inclusion and equity, we have yet to find the centre. We need new remedies as a global community. *The Infinite Leader* is such a remedy. Chris Lewis and Pippa Malmgren provide us with new strategies to bring the pendulum into alignment.

All my life, I've been in pursuit of balance. In our quest, professional women must articulate both the language of the workplace with that of family management. Educators are especially aware of the need to balance the pressures placed upon students with allowing them to become the best version of themselves. I have a particular appreciation for the demands of both spheres.

As an educator, it is an invaluable text for understanding the ways in which education can better position students for success in the workplace. Traditional notions of success and achievement are turned on their head. *The Infinite Leader* requires that attitude and a collaborative spirit be considered as meaningfully as quantitative analysis and data sets by the modern leader. The interrogatives posed throughout the text allow the reader to find relevance in their own personal leadership arc. Much like Viktor Frankl's *Man's Search for Meaning*, which requires that the reader deeply self-reflect, *The Infinite Leader* demands an inner journey – a new approach to modern leadership.

Imbalance is all around us and it's growing. It's seen in our physical environment throughout the globe with rising temperatures, social unrest and pandemics. It's evident in our politics, where people struggle to engage in reasonable discourse and the loudest, most extreme voices seem to prevail. It's seen in our approach to capital, its management and deployment. A world off balance is perhaps the greatest issue of our age.

In *The Infinite Leader*, Chris and Pippa lay out a wide ranging thesis on leadership covering economics, gender, philosophy and education. It is designed to be read by people from all walks of life because its message is universal. It lays out an analysis of leadership models to date and proposes a new approach and philosophy. Blending insights on subjects such as religious faith, cybermancy, zeronomics, modern politics and gender, this book shatters our notion of traditional business tomes. Brilliantly written and highly accessible, *The Infinite Leader* is an invitation to true self-reflection for the modern leader. Replete with references to great thinkers and intriguing ideologies, the book is itself a treatise on valuing 'the quality of thought'.

Inez Robinson-Odom
Assistant Principal at Academy of Our Lady of Peace
San Diego

Acknowledgements

Sarah Aitchison, Sarah Aitchison
and Sarah Aitchison
Helen Alderson
Lori Ames
Shazia Amin
Sinclair Beecham
Simon Billington
Mark Borkowski
Professor David Brown
Lord Chadlington
Nadia Chand
Viv Church
Géraldine Collard
Professor Sir Cary Cooper
Alison Cork
Chris Cudmore
Francis Davis
Peter De Haan
Jacqueline de Rojas
Emma Draude
Umang Dokey
Noah Dye
Ken Ford
Professor Russell Foster
Steve Frampton
Jaini Haria
Cherylyn Harley LeBon
Robert J Herbold
Lord Holmes of Richmond
Amir Hussain
Baroness Anne Jenkin

Edmund V King
Helen Kogan
Gary Krahn
Sir Geoffrey Leigh
Richard Levick
Jo Lewis
Pip Lewis
Georgia Lewis
Charlotte Lindsey Curtet
Andy Martinus
Lord Mawson
Megan Maguire
Rt Hon Penny Mordant MP
Ella Miller
Lance Nail
James Oehlcke
Wes Paul
Peter Pereira Gray
Milenko Prvacki
Kelly Redding
Tom Savigar
John Paul Schutte
Sir Anthony Seldon
Ellis Taylor
Arthur Thompson
Bill Thornhill
Kenneth Todorov
Yvonne van Bokhoven
Greg Williamson
Sir George Zambellas

Introduction

In years to come, people should be able to look back at 2020 and say it was the year that changed everything. There's no doubt it will hold more than the usual memories. It was a vivid experience, where everything became heightened and exaggerated. If there was ever a time when leadership could be seen and assessed, this was it. Better than any MBA or training course, at both individual and group level, this was leadership put to the test repeatedly and relentlessly.

Our leadership has failed us again. As we prepared to publish this book, much of the world was in lockdown in response to the COVID-19 pandemic. The world economy has ceased functioning by any normal measure. The virus has revealed how deeply indebted, leveraged and fragile the world economy is. Meanwhile, it is ever clearer that leaders have once again been surprised and wrong-footed. Whatever trust the public had left in them has been damaged yet again.

The biggest tragedy of what turned out to be a catastrophic year could be that we learn nothing from the experience. So, in what should be a new era, this book asks questions.

How do you feel about leaders? Do they represent your views? Do they work in your interest? Do they look and sound like you? Do they understand you? Have they had similar experiences to you? Are they interested in the long term? Or are they ruled by short-term numbers? Are they looking after your world? Will your children thank them for their farsightedness? Do our leaders envisage and bring to life infinite possibilities or do they make do with the idea that all options are limited?

You've picked up this book because you want some answers. You want the right answers. You want certainty. Who should I follow? Who should I listen to? Who's smart? Which leaders should I choose? How can I get more of what I want from my leaders? How can I be a better leader? Why are the leaders we choose so flawed?

This book builds upon the success of the award-winning *The Leadership Lab*. The authors are a British subject living in the US and a US citizen living in London, who advise leaders all over the world, a man and a woman who both bring a global view. The research is compiled from hundreds of interviews and consulting clients from all around the world, and many different industries and occupations. It is an up-to-date contemporary analysis.

While writing this book and discussing it with clients, we were struck by the commonality of the question, 'Who should we follow?' We joke that it is like a scene from the film *The Life of Brian*, where the crowd is looking for a sign of God. One character holds up a sandal and everyone says 'It's a sign! Follow him!' In other words, we are all looking for a simple sign that will help us choose our leader. It shows one thing – that we all really believe there is a simple, correct, universal answer, but the reality is even simpler still. It resides in each of us to become better leaders and have a better understanding of leadership.

Our answer is to follow the most balanced leader who demonstrates an infinite range, playing all the notes of leadership. Yes, we want profitability but with understanding and compassion, too. We don't just want leaders to be 'Zen'. We want them to be *Zen*, as well as full of energy, dynamism, defiance, logic and emotion. This is what we mean by the Infinite Leader. When we measure them on a balance, we don't want them to be +1 or –1. We don't want them to be –9 or +4. We want them to be capable of ALL numbers but based at zero. More about this later.

There are plenty of books on leadership, but many are underwhelming. That happens when they are written by people who haven't led but are happy to share their opinions. Of course, this is not to say their opinions don't count. It is to say that understanding leadership is far more profound when it is felt and experienced. This is not to say you particularly need to be a technical expert to lead. We're talking about the leadership of people here. There are many different approaches and styles for as many different situations. But there are commonalities. For instance, leadership cannot occur without followership. Leaders do not exist by themselves.

Leadership books are overwhelmingly written by men. This fails to include or parenthesize half the team. Many are written solely by westerners who score leaders based on financial performance or votes rather than on their ability to reframe problems and to bring people together. Many leadership books are rooted in a single culture, even a single leader. They often focus on Western business or military culture.

Always remember we are the ones that choose our leaders. Before we go into an organization, how often do we study the leadership, their background, experience, diversity, even their financial performance? It's up to us to vote with our feet, and we will. That's when we can show leadership ourselves. We are part of leadership. It is a mistake to believe that the only leaders in our society are the ones with designated titles like president, prime minister or CEO. We look around and feel we regularly see more leadership outside of that traditional definition. For example, in a single-parent household we see at least as much fiscal discipline, planning and motivation as we see in corporations, and possibly more. This leadership is often delivered under more trying circumstances with a lot less resource than any government or private company. We are all part of the leadership class and this is part of the answer to the leadership question. Our own choices and behaviours can mould the future. We have the power to be and to choose better leaders.

We know that leadership is emotive. We can love or hate our leaders and hold them responsible. First though, we must learn to take control and hold ourselves responsible, as in the words of 'Invictus' by William Henley.[1]

Out of the night that covers me,
Black as the pit from pole to pole,
I thank whatever gods may be
For my unconquerable soul.

In the fell clutch of circumstance
I have not winced nor cried aloud.
Under the bludgeonings of chance
My head is bloody, but unbowed.

Beyond this place of wrath and tears
Looms but the Horror of the shade,
And yet the menace of the years
Finds and shall find me unafraid.

It matters not how strait the gate,
How charged with punishments the scroll,
I am the master of my fate,
I am the captain of my soul.

We can't always change our leaders or our circumstances, but we can change our response to them.

Words are sometimes inadequate to describe the way we feel about leadership. We find our leaders exasperating. Leadership in every part of our society and in every part of the world has been failing. This was true before the onset of the pandemic in

2020. There is little doubt that many individual leaders are flawed, but there's something bigger going on. The pervasiveness of leadership catastrophes across the world in almost every possible kind of organization tells us that the problem is now systemic.

This is especially true in the world of politics, where divisions and opinions about leaders can be so diametrically opposed as to be irreconcilable. But here, we should have faith in our democratic systems. If we get the wrong leader in our view, then there are always options to change them next time.

It would be easy to become cynical about leadership failure, because many of the reasons are clear. Our leaders often seem to be complacent or out of touch or taken by surprise. They are neither balanced personally nor balancing the competing interests of the public they serve. Leadership has become too focused on the short term, too tactical, quantitative, narrow and self-interested. Worse, our leaders have great certainty that they are right. Mediocrity can be the only provenance of this type of certainty. If leadership is convinced that this is the best it can be and there's no more improvement to come, then that isn't leadership.

The response to leadership failure has been a crescendo of objection and protest from voters, investors, employees, activists, students, even schoolchildren. Yet it doesn't need to be like this. There is a way to rebalance leadership. It involves a change in behaviour and in the way that we view and choose our leaders. The problem is not, as many believe, that there is poor leadership. Often, there is no leadership visible at all. In many instances, leadership isn't even discussed as an issue that threatens us. Partly, leadership seems to have its own narrative about who to blame. This often focuses on environmental factors, for example a recession or unforeseen circumstances. But there is usually no talk of the role that leadership played in it.

We also make the mistake of confusing leadership with management. The two are related, but they are not the same.

Here, a great deal of time and money is invested in management training. Management is about doing things right. That's not the same as doing the right things. That's what we call leadership. There is a moral dimension too, which is often wilfully ignored. We don't recruit people on the basis of their belief systems or their morality. We often just assume them to be congruent with our own. Or, we assume that confidence is the same as competence. It is not. As we shall see.

The current heads of our organizations are intelligent. Indeed, many have undergone decades of education in schools, universities and professional institutes. But our leaders have had a narrow education focused on a particular type of thinking, which resolves problems by analysis. In other words, by breaking them down. This leads to a 'drill-down' philosophy that is used for everything. When you only have a hammer, every problem is a nail. This is having catastrophic effects on collective endeavour. Organizations that have been set up as logical structures suddenly find themselves unable to adapt, because they are too siloed by the divisions they imposed upon themselves as part of their structure. Organizations and brands are suffering and so are the stakeholders and the environment itself.

Why has leadership become so much more important recently? This is because of what Professor Marek Korczynski at the University of Nottingham calls 'service work'.[2] All advanced economies are now dominated by service industries. Over 10 per cent of the UK workforce is employed in the retail sector and more now work in doctors' offices than in car plants, in laundries and dry cleaners than in steel mills.

The move away from manufacturing and agriculture towards service industries in advanced economies is continuing.[3] Between 1974 and 1994, service sector employment rose by 9 per cent to 73 per cent in the USA, by 13 per cent to 71 per cent in Australia, and from 50 per cent to 60 per cent in Japan.[4] Not only have more people moved into services, but many of these have moved into direct customer contact roles. This places much more emphasis on interpersonal skills and team leadership rather than simple industrial technique. More knowledge work means more workers with knowledge and a more sophisticated, skilled and expensive team. Leadership is therefore critical to the efficiency and leveraging of the investment.

To be a knowledge worker is, in itself, to be unbalanced. The roles are often sedentary, intellectually intensive and stressful.

That's why this book focuses on balance. It's the infinite challenge. At the root of it is the way we each prepare for responsibility. Leadership tries actively to avoid the extremes, almost as if the requirement for ultraperformance is a sign of failure. But how are leaders to develop their skills and the capabilities of their teams if they always stay within limits? Pushing the boundaries is important for efficiency, but it's possible only where there is a clear sense of balance. It's because balance between extremes allows leadership to draw upon all eventualities, rather than just an over-reliance on one.

It stands to reason that agility must be founded upon balance. Being centrally located always provides the shortest and fastest distance to reach any extreme. This demands that we understand that we are not faced with just one set of extremes. There are multiple continua and each can be intersected to investigate the balance point.

For instance, this means balancing skills between the short and long term. Between the quantitative and the qualitative. Between the masculine and feminine – not just the male and female. Between the tactical and the strategic. Between the needs of the individual and those of the team. Between the local and the global. Between innovation and the status quo. Between the emotional and the rational. Between the physical and spiritual.

This idea for a 'zero' approach came from studying Cartesian coordinates, with intersecting axes. These are made up of two continua, which represent extremes. Normally, the origin of the graph is set at zero, but we realized that the zero point could be reinterpreted as a balance point or fulcrum. A zero is also a kind of symbolic portal where we can transform today's reality into potentially infinite possibilities.

The development of the axes was based on research and draws upon history, economics, politics, social and physical science, mathematics, philosophy and psychology. At the heart of the Infinite Leader idea is what we've called the zero model of leadership, which shows how leadership can be rebalanced. Of course, balance is something seldom achieved and, in that respect, is infinite.

This balance point is important in the theory and is best illustrated by a 3D perspective where there is a vanishing point. This is the equilibrium point that great leadership inhabits – just far enough away to be seeing the future but with a presence in the here and now. The vanishing point in any picture is the place where perspective lines converge and the landscape beyond is out of view. This is the infinity point. This is the zone in which the leader needs to operate. They need to transcend the landscape with true situational fluency. This means an awareness of where we are, where we've been and where we're trying to get to, and what might stop us.

We became fascinated with the idea that great leadership was capable of going to any extreme required but consistently returning to balance. After all, the balance point offers the shortest deployment distance to meet any extreme challenge. Too many leaders get dragged into firefighting in the present. The leader's job is to do what everyone else is unwilling or unable to do. They try to avoid duplicating effort because they have unique skills or experience. Too many leaders have to kick every ball. This is why they need to develop the ability to zoom out. This is not to say they should be zoomed out at all times. The Infinite Leader is one who can operate at the extreme of each axis. But in aggregate, they are based at zero, where they will return before moving back to the extremes.

We've organized this book to make some simple points. First, that we've reached a turning point in leadership. We're seeing the final stage of an unbalanced approach, which uses short-term efficiency as an excuse for long-term damage and waste of resources in the form of people, capital and our environment. Second, that we must see the imbalance in the great sweep of history, which has been a struggle to leaven faith with logic and science and to achieve a more balanced approach. This has progressed too far, to a new imbalance and over-reliance on analytic logic. Third, that if we can understand what the balance means, it can make us more creative, productive, fair and long-term effective.

Chapter 1, The end, describes the level and extent of leadership failure, its consequences and causes. Chapter 2, Circles and zeros, narrates the history of imbalance and reminds us how closely aligned zero and infinite possibility have been in our culture and history. In Chapter 3, Existing leadership models, we explain how our management thinking brought us here and the evolution of leadership models. Chapter 4 introduces the infinite model and explains how each quadrant balances the other. We take the first model, 'hearts and minds', and explain it in detail. Chapter 5 deals with the philosophy of balanced or 'zero'-state thinking. This explains the complexity of dealing with trends that seem to be paradoxical or superpositioned. They can be both one thing and another. So, for instance, information can bring insight. Too much can bring blindness. Chapter 6 examines the nature of a superior society and the implications of zero thinking on economics. Zeronomics explores how economics is changing. It suggests that to re-engineer our leadership, we also need to adopt an almost existential approach to budgets. This is where 'What if?' thinking comes in. What if we were going to start from a blank sheet of paper? What if we were just starting up? How would we do this? Supposing we didn't have this budget, what level of budget would be needed (zero-based budgeting)? Zero leadership thinking doesn't require capital. It uses its 'convening' power to identify alignments. This is what we've termed 'zero ego, zero gender'. We tackle this in Chapter 7.

Closely linked to this is Chapter 8, Zero education. This describes the inadequate ways we prepare for leadership. It describes the methods of scoring in school, in university, at work, which have nothing to do with collaboration, empathy and teamwork. It addresses the need for fresh thinking in education, imagination and creativity.

Chapter 9 explores where the thinking takes us. Wherever you find people taking responsibility, you will find love in the form of duty. This applies especially to the family. The act of caring for a child or for an elderly parent is born out of love. Wherever you find responsibility you will find leadership. This covers the four Hs of servant leadership: humble, happy, honest and hungry.

The final section concludes and summarizes the book. It explores several paradoxes, for instance how we can have so much data but be so blind, and how we can be better educated than ever but still be so ignorant. It investigates equality and draws links between the behaviour of many of our leaders and some of the opportunities as well as problems this creates.

At this time, still in the shadow of one of the greatest events in the lives of all of us, we wanted to advance leadership thinking with this book. So, we had to take a risk and do something different. We wanted to really think through what would give us better leadership. We hope that what we discovered on the way surprises you as much as it surprised us.

The opportunity for improvement is within all of us. That may explain why it remains so elusive – it's the last place we would ever think of looking for it.

Chris Lewis
Pippa Malmgren
May 2020

CHAPTER ONE

The end

How bad is the current leadership situation? To what extent has leadership failed and in what areas? Why did it happen? What were its causes? What was the financial cost of this failure? How did it change our culture? Is it just that we hear a lot more about leadership failure because it's more visible?

We live in an age of catastrophic leadership failure. In 2020 coronavirus struck millions of people around the world, creating a global recession and massive disruption. For those lucky enough to escape it, the impact was still felt in fear, isolation and anxiety. There have been multiple failures of international cooperation, in the sharing of resources and the preparation for the event. If the first duty of leadership is to protect the community, then at best it has mitigated the outcome. At worst, it has failed to protect the weakest and most vulnerable in our community.

Some will say it could have been worse. This will fall upon deaf ears with many groups. With those who lost loved ones before their time. With those who lost their careers, homes and opportunities. With those who were left in great anxiety who will never feel confident again.

What can be learned from this? Our primary conclusion is that our priorities have become inverted. The resulting lack of balance has been costly. The biggest mistake would be for us to emerge from this and to continue, unchanged. Now is the time for a wholesale review of our leadership to see how it could be improved.

But the failure is not just represented in the management and leadership during a pandemic. The problem was there before that. In 2018, more CEOs were forced out of office for ethical lapse than for any other reason.[1] The research showed that turnover in the role of CEO increased to an all-time high of 17.5 per cent churn or an average stay of just over five years. The research suggested that now, more than ever, today's leaders seem to have lost their moral compass. Ethical lapse points to a lack of judgement. So what? Why does it matter? Because it destroys people's faith, their values, their wealth and even hope itself.

In 2018, more CEOs were forced out of office for ethical lapse than for any other reason.

What is an ethical leader?

There are lots of ways of defining what it means to be an ethical leader, but it boils down to the following:

- respecting people;
- building a community;
- demonstrating justice;
- serving others;
- being honest.

You wouldn't think this was difficult, would you? You'd think that this would fall into the category of leadership basics. So, we need to ask what might warp these principles.

The most obvious factor is the focus on short-term financials. This is particularly exacerbated in companies that are quoted in the US for instance, where the reporting is quarterly. This sometimes leads to chasing performance numbers rather than focusing on customer service.

Another factor might be too rigid a leadership style, which permits only certain outcomes. If the leader is in a hurry to move on to the next thing, then they are likely to bring in their own team, which can sometimes result in a lack of understanding of commitments made.

New leadership sometimes believes that getting to know a community is a waste of time. But, without listening, the leader can run into resistance. Sometimes, cultures are really looking forward to change and they can be fully cooperative with new leaders.

Ethical leadership shouldn't mean you are less dynamic, or even less dedicated and focused on objectives. It does matter, though, how you do these things.

The upward trend in unethical behaviour suggests that some leaders simply don't care how something is done, as long as it gets done. Some may even be engaging directly in unethical behaviour themselves. Even if the leader isn't misbehaving, they can still be promoting it unwittingly. The phrase to follow is: 'The tone begins at the top.'

It comes down to what the leader 'is' rather than what they 'do'.

This tone is set by the way the leader rewards, condones or ignores employees' behaviour. This sets a clear benchmark for what behaviour will be valued. The leader doesn't even need to do anything. For evil to persist, good people need do nothing. It comes down to what the leader 'is' rather than what they 'do'.

This is what we said in *The Leadership Lab* (reproduced with kind permission of Kogan Page):

> Since the turn of the century, we've learned that our leaders have illegally avoided taxes,[2] lied about emissions in the car

industry,[3] rigged interest rates,[4] laundered Mexican drug money,[5] presided over an offshore banking system that was larger than anyone thought possible,[6] forced good companies into closure[7] and destroyed pension funds as they themselves grew wealthier.[8] Collectively, they oversaw unprecedented destruction of wealth and the collapse of the financial system[9] and watched as life savings placed into investment funds set up by leaders of unimpeachable integrity turned out to be Ponzi schemes.[10] Our spiritual leaders have covered up sex abuse in the Church.[11] Our charity leaders have sexually abused the vulnerable.[12] Our entertainment leaders are facing multiple allegations of sexual harassment and abuse.[13] Our leading broadcasters have falsely accused political figures of being child abusers,[14] while allowing actual abusers to commit crimes on their premises.[15] Meanwhile, sporting leaders have been caught cheating and doping.[16] Our medical leaders have chronically mistreated patients.[17] Even the US President's political advisors are being jailed[18] and there are calls to impeach the leader of the free world.

From the Mossack Fonseca and Paradise Papers revelations, it's estimated[19] that $8.7 trillion, or 11 per cent, of global wealth resides in tax havens.[20] Governments may have created the conditions for tax havens, but it is only now that we have begun to understand the consequences of these policies. Shielding that money deprived world governments of approximately $170 billion in tax revenue in 2016 alone, with the United States Treasury taking a hit of $32 billion that it might otherwise have had. Most felt the problems were mitigated because this offshore financial system was a fraction of the individual onshore economies. It turned out to be a multiple of them.

These events sound fantastic, incredible, unbelievable, even impossible, but they happened and continue to happen. They didn't just call into question discrete leadership cultures, but the whole system. The collapse of trust on this scale, even 10 years later, is still being felt.

The conclusion must be that our problems with leadership are not professional but behavioural. When a five-year-old misbehaves at a party, the criterion applied for removal by a watchful parent must be the point at which harm to their peers becomes likely. Of course, we can't expect an errant child to comply with the intervention. It's more likely to be the opposite. More than 10 years after the great recession, which began in 2007, there has been no tantrum because there has still been no punishment. Worse still, the response to the problem of making money too freely available is to increase its availability still further, with predictable consequences.

The power of capital versus the power of people

Some might argue that the greedy short-termism that we've seen create so much destruction is just the way of the capitalist world. They would argue that minority groups are having little impact on mainstream leadership culture. But is that true? Some of the biggest changes have been brought about by minority groups such as the Tea Party, Extinction Rebellion, the MeToo movement, Black Lives Matter and minority shareholders. In fact, you could argue that all modern progressive development has always been delivered by minority groups.

The point here is that the power of capital and of minority groups could be made even greater by recognizing that their causes are one and the same. Leadership failure has a massive cost, and not just financial. One of the biggest costs could be in the loss of faith that we have in the capital and political process itself. No one is seriously contemplating scrapping democracies, but many would point out that the communist system appears to be much more successful economically (at least in the short term). How often do we now hear that authoritarian economies perform better, faster and more fairly than capitalist systems?

The relevant point about leadership is that it should actively be seeking out minority views, because they may provide a vital early warning system. This was illustrated several times by the great financial crash of 2007–2009. There were voices that were concerned about confidence, liquidity and the validity of the US mortgage market, but no one listened because they were dismissed as maverick. Raghuram Rajan, an economist from India, presented a paper at the annual meeting of central bankers in Jackson Hole, Wyoming, in 2005 where he warned of an imminent financial crisis. He was right. But his views were dismissed at the time.[21] He went on to become the Governor of the central bank in India in September 2013. The very definition of maverick might be 'not the majority', but this could also describe leadership itself.

Leadership needs to listen to these maverick voices, not because they're always right, but because they're always different. The leader's job is not to predict one outcome and prepare for it. It's to prepare for all outcomes. What matters is having the imagination to see the potential outcomes and include them in the planning process.

This, incidentally, is not also just for the black swan moment of catastrophe but also for routine innovation. After all, if someone has a view that's out there, could it be that they're just 'early' in the innovation process? If that's the case then it becomes not a matter of if, but simply when.

What did these failures cost?

These failures have a cost. We have yet to understand the true cost of the COVID-19-led economic crisis, though some are already arguing that it will eventually be even bigger than the financial crisis.[22] While politicians focus on growth and development of the economy, the cost of the financial crisis alone was estimated at $22 trillion.[23] That's $70,000 for every single

American. Of course, you can point to the fact that the stock markets hit new highs in 2019, but that tells you the value of shares now. It doesn't tell you what they *could* have been (see Figure 1.1).[24]

The US Government Accountability Office[25] said:

> Research suggests that US output losses associated with the 2007–2009 financial crisis could range from several trillion to over $10 trillion. In January 2012, the Congressional Budget Office (CBO) estimated that the cumulative difference between actual GDP and estimated potential GDP following the crisis would amount to $5.7 trillion by 2018.

These numbers sound big but to put them into context, $1 trillion would buy you Apple. $22 trillion would wipe out US national debt.[26] The US Government brings in about $3.1 trillion every year but is currently spending $4.1 trillion.[27] The annual deficit is heading for $1 trillion. This is just the annual gap every year between what the US earns and what it spends. It grew 17 per cent between 2017 and 2018 alone.

FIGURE 1.1 Real GDP

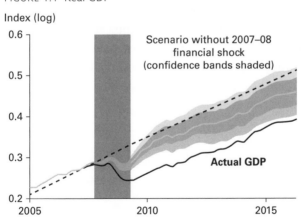

Source: FRBSF Economic Letter 2018

For any students of economics out there, this level of deficit-funded expansion tends to be inflationary, or at least asset inflationary. It's potentially one reason why the stock markets keep going from one record high to another. Similar pressures are occurring in most other economies in the world today.[28] The point here is that the financial recklessness is continuing. Had it not been for the financial crisis, we can say that most governments would have been able to double their spending in one year. Alternatively, they could have substantially increased budgets on public services over a longer period of time.

The financial cost alone of the leadership failure is monstrous. And that's just in finance. And that's before we take account of the pandemic. If we added the costs of leadership failure in other sectors, the social cost would be higher still.

Non-financial costs

So, we can assess roughly what this level of leadership failure is costing in monetary terms, but what else is at stake? This is harder to quantify, but no less devastating. According to a Harris Poll of young Americans, asked what their goal in life was, one answer came back. It was not to be happy in their work or fulfilled in their domestic life. The number one goal for 94 per cent of them was to be debt-free.[29] If accurate, this is a depressing finding for a whole generation.

The rising tide of anger

On just about every scale that can be measured, anger is increasing.[30] Does this represent a lack of self-control or discipline? Or perhaps the want of an organized, institutional outlet for it? Or perhaps such a fulfilment of needs that anger has become recreational outrage in the manner of virtue signalling?[31] [32]

It is certainly tangible and measurable. It can be seen in the frustration with political results and also with public services. One-third of all NHS nurses have been attacked at work. The Royal College of Nursing recorded a 9.7 per cent increase in attacks on its staff.[33] One-quarter of all teachers have experienced violence from students.[34] The British Association of Anger Management[35] says almost a third of people have trouble controlling their anger. Almost half of us regularly lose our temper at work and confess to 'office rage'. The majority of absences from work are caused by stress. One-third of British people are not on speaking terms with their neighbours. There were 10,854 air rage[36] incidents reported by airlines worldwide in 2016, up from 9,316 incidents in 2014. The UK has the second-worst road rage in the world after South Africa.[37] More than 80 per cent of drivers say they have been involved in road rage incidents and 25 per cent have committed an act of road rage themselves. 71 per cent of internet users admit to having suffered internet rage. 50 per cent of us have reacted to computer problems by hitting our PC, hurling parts of it around and/or abusing colleagues. More than one-third of the UK population is losing sleep from anxiety.[38]

This is not just a one off. According to Gallup's annual US survey, in 2019 Americans experienced stress, anger and worry at levels surpassing those seen over the past decade.[39] The majority (55 per cent) reported feelings of high stress. US stress levels were higher than the global average of 35 per cent. Failure at the top is felt more strongly at the bottom of society.

Impact on culture

We're still working through this great tragedy in our popular culture. We're still trying to work out what happened and why. We've had plays about the Lehman Brothers[40] and Enron.[41] Books like *Too Big to Fail*,[42] *Crashed*,[43] *Lords of Finance*,[44] *All the Devils Are Here,*[45] *Crisis Economics,*[46] *Makers and Takers,*[47] *The End of Wall Street*[48] and *Crash of the Titans*[49] all explore this. Films like *The Big Short*[50] and *The Laundromat*[51] dramatize the effect. This is still recent history, now overtaken by a new crisis that may further postpone confident conclusions.

The big problem is that we're looking for rational explanations to explain irrational behaviour. This is the level of inadequacy in our analysis.

Let's start with who we put in charge to take responsibility. Perhaps the most truly staggering consideration here is that none of these leaders thought they would end up in this situation. They could not even conceive of the scale of the catastrophe. This suggests a distinct lack of imagination for what could happen, or perhaps how fast things could be reframed.

If it was known that Catholic priests were abusing boys, why did no one address that? Could it be that it was so fantastic as to be unbelievable? How about Hollywood and its sexual exploitation? Surely we knew that was a thing? How about banks laundering drug money? Did they not know? Perhaps they chose not to look too closely? Perhaps they operated from within such a narrow value set that it was only the reframing in retrospect that repositioned them?

As Edmund Burke put it: 'The only thing necessary for the triumph of evil is for good men to do nothing.'[52] The tragic thing about the collapse in leadership is that many knew. But they failed to act. Everyone who benefited didn't want to rock the boat. The public response has been palpable. It can be likened to the grief cycle:[53]

Denial → Anger → Depression → Bargaining → (Cynical) Acceptance

The only problem with this model is that far from ending in a steady state, the cycle repeats and deepens with each new breach of trust. At each stage, we're willing to try ever more extreme ideas to fix it. We've been here before in history. Maybe time for a strong leader? Curtail civil and human rights? Let's elect someone who can just smash everything up.

This has led to a splintering that many authors have sought to explain. Matthew Goodwin and Roger Eatwell[54] have called it a revolt against liberal democracy. James Reeves[55] categorized it as the difference between 'Anywheres' and 'Somewheres', the latter (and vast majority of Americans) being those who live within 20 miles of where they were born.

However the problem is defined and identified, it is very real and growing. According to Pew Research,[56] we're more divided than we ever have been in history. The resulting anger sometimes bemuses the liberal mind. Surely, we are all reasonable people? Can't we have patient dialogue? Of course we can. The urgency for us to deal with the situations listed above is becoming acute and it's not going to be fixed quickly. The situation has built up over time, and like a mighty river it has multiple tributaries, as we shall see.

This split of angry people bears some investigation. Anger begets anger. But anger is based on fear. What are they afraid of? Put simply, people are angry that their world is changing in ways they don't like. They're angry at the people who are angry at them. The anger on both sides is understandable and compounded by rapid change.

But how *new* is any of this?

There is intergenerational anger between older people who feel that younger people are feckless and have not had to endure what they've had to. In truth, this is hardly new. Socrates, who lived from 469 to 399 BC, said: 'The children now love luxury; they have bad manners, contempt for authority; they show disrespect for elders and love chatter in place of exercise. Children are now tyrants, not the servants of their households. They no longer rise when elders enter the room. They contradict their parents, chatter before company, gobble up dainties at the table, cross their legs, and tyrannize their teachers.'[57]

There is interracial anger, as illustrated by the 'Black Lives Matter' campaign. This is hardly new either. The Black Panthers were an angry manifestation of the Civil Rights Movement in the 1960s. There is political anger between the current incumbent of the White House and the Democratic Party, but the anger with Richard Nixon over the Vietnam War was of an equivalence. There is anger between Brexiteers and Remainers in the UK, but is this anger or violence greater than three world wars (two hot, one cold) that began in Europe and engulfed the world?

The difference now is the sheer scale of it. Good leadership is now the exception rather than the rule. On top of this, we cannot say they did not know. Their job is to know. That's what we have leaders for.

Could it be they had a sense of powerlessness? That they felt they couldn't do anything about it. Were they too tenured in their roles that they feared the repercussions? Could it be that as people have become relaxed about judging some behaviours, they have relaxed all judgement? For instance, when did it become OK to cheat at sport? We've seen this time and time again, in soccer, in cycling, in cricket and in rugby. Have the prizes for winning become too great? Have the temptations to cut corners become too enticing?

Management of perception, not reality

The other difference is that the traditional sources of information are no longer trusted. The multiplicity of sources and pressure to produce stories as fast as possible means a lot of inaccuracy. The speed of the story has always been inverse to the truth. Again, the difference here is that some of the manipulation at least is no longer imperative-induced mistake. It's more likely to be cynicism-induced mischief. One of the best examples of this is the recent phenomenon of deepfake videos. This is where video is deliberately manipulated to create a specific effect. A video of US Speaker Nancy Pelosi was changed to make her sound drunk. Technology now allows anyone, even a president, to be shown to be saying words that they never actually said. This sort of false signal hides in plain view. With the advent of artificial intelligence, the manipulation techniques become so sophisticated that they become indistinguishable from the reality.

The honest, though, tend not to use fake news to enhance their message. Only the wrongdoers will. Sadly, those with a better story will get the attention.

Who's to blame?

When we do not trust each other, we are more isolated than ever before. Leadership is supposed to bring us together. In every area, it seems to be doing the opposite. We can blame our leaders, but that is unlikely to help. We are all leaders now and therefore we all have responsibility.

We have to ask some questions: 'In our lifetimes, will subsequent generations say of us that we tried to work together for mutual benefit, with our long-term futures in mind? Will they say we looked after the weak? Will they say we were unselfish, frugal and well meaning? What will they say of me? Will they say you did the best with what you had, that you always sought balance? That you always treated people in a way you would have liked to have been treated?'

Leadership must be a moral commitment to do the right thing or it's nothing.

How do you rebuild trust?

This is a well-trodden path and it involves admitting fault, accepting responsibility, asking for forgiveness, changing behaviour and actively working to rebuild trust. How many signs of this have you seen from the banking, political, petrochemical and religious communities that failed so greatly? It hasn't happened. In many instances, the attention has simply moved on to other areas.

This leaves huge opportunities for other brands that recognize the problem and step in to provide the community with something better. This is happening, as people move away from brands that they see as acting unethically. So for instance, the Royal Shakespeare Company (RSC) said it was dropping the oil company BP's long-term sponsorship, a week after schools wrote to the organization threatening a boycott.[58] Schools called upon the RSC to end its partnership with the oil firm and threatened to protest if action was not taken. BP had been sponsoring the theatre company's £5 discounted tickets for 16–25-year-olds since 2013.

The letter from the schools said:

> These sponsorship deals allow BP to pretend that it cares about young people by giving them the chance to be inspired by amazing live performances and kindle a lifelong love of theatre. In reality, BP is jeopardizing the futures of these young people they apparently care so much about, by continuing to extract huge quantities of oil and gas, and actively lobbying against the climate change policies that we school strikers are pushing so hard for.

In a statement, RSC Directors Gregory Doran and Catherine Mallyon said:

> Amidst the climate emergency, which we recognise, young people are now saying clearly to us that the BP sponsorship is putting a barrier between them and their wish to engage with the RSC. We cannot ignore that message.

Consumer press is also growing. *Ethical Consumer* magazine has over 6,000 subscribers, more than 15,000 recipients of its weekly emails and its website attracts over 120,000 unique visitors per month.

Around the world, minority groups are reasserting their values and banding together to remind leaders that things have become out of balance.

Recognizing the issues

We know good leaders, even great leaders, are out there. Leaders with integrity, courage and wisdom. Inclusive leaders. Leaders who change the lives of the many. Leaders who think. Leaders who join the dots. The best modern leaders become so by studying the worst. Studying failure might strike some as being an odd use of their time but most leaders will tell you they learn more from failure than they do from success. In fact, so much progress depends upon failure to provide the incentive for change.

What do the cataclysmic events listed earlier have in common? Did they lack professionally qualified university-educated leaders? No. So, why didn't they notice what was happening? Were they distracted by too much or too little information? Did they know they were doing wrong? Did they lack the imagination to see the effects of this? Did they feel they couldn't speak out? Did they think they would just get away with it? Did their size play a part? Did it matter that they were led mainly by middle-aged men? If there were women in senior positions, did they just fall into a male culture and start behaving in the same way? What role did technology play? Are there clear patterns here?

The best modern leaders become so by studying the worst.

There was clearly motivation and determination, but *to do wrong* or at least to wilfully ignore the right thing. These things didn't happen by accident, but nor was it one single event that caused them. Whether they did not intend it or whether it was apparent by subsequent reframing, it is bad leadership. It is unbalanced in just about every way. It is these imbalances that we must study. Let's look at some here.

Rapid change – no ability to balance past and future

At best, our leadership has been outpaced by rapid change. Culturally, technically and therefore geopolitically, our leaders and their institutions have been overwhelmed by change.

This has led to 'economic rationalism' being lauded as the single objective of leadership even at the expense of ethical behaviour. This, in turn, has given us the 'superlative' (as opposed to the 'superior') economy. The biggest is the best. If leadership confines itself to economic rationalism, it will always be suboptimal because it will always choose quantitative over qualitative criteria.

Information overload – inability to balance information

In an age obsessed with now, the past is disrespected and dismissed. The present is what matters. Why has this changed so much? This can be tracked directly to the smartphone and the level of distraction and overload caused by the sheer volume of interruptions and data. If the average person receives 40 emails a day and the average day is 8 hours or 480 minutes, then we're interrupted every 12 minutes.[59]

On top of this failure (and perhaps as a contributory cause of it), we're overloaded with more information than ever before. We have so much information that we have become blinded to the obvious facts that are front and centre. We live in an age of instant entertainment so much more compelling than the truth. We have become atomized and the mystery of the bigger picture is hidden from us, despite being in plain view.

Then there is the knowledge doubling curve. The famed engineer Buckminster Fuller realized that the volume of information and human knowledge was rising exponentially in the 20th century. He noticed that before the 20th century, human knowledge doubled approximately every 250 years. After 1900, it began to double every 100 years. By the end of World War II, knowledge was doubling every 25 years. By 1982, Fuller estimated that human knowledge was doubling every year (Figure 1.2). IBM says knowledge is now doubling every 12 hours.[60] The addition of Internet of Things devices is only accelerating this extraordinary avalanche of data.

This Doubling Curve[61] helps explain why people are feeling uneasy. They cannot keep up. No one can read fast enough to take in the new information, let alone make sense of it. It becomes easier to distinguish between useful and useless information simply by assessing who said it, then dismissing the source. Some grant reliability to information, if it comes from the Democrats or CNN. Others grant that to the Republican Party and Fox News. Back in the late 1960s, Marshall McLuhan anticipated this avalanche and predicted that information overload would tend to make us more tribal.[62] Leaders today need to understand that there is ever less actual understanding. Rather than arriving at an informed opinion, people are less bothered now by facts. Faith has become a bigger driver of opinions than logic.

FIGURE 1.2 Buckminster Fuller's Knowledge Doubling Curve

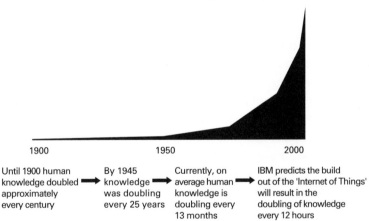

Source: Blake, D (2015) The learning economy: 5 global trends every CLO should be watching, Degreed Inc

Information should flow as a process. If it doesn't, information becomes an event. We need to parse and balance information flow so it illuminates, rather than obscures, the path ahead.

Lack of consequence – the wrongdoers go unpunished

A common symbol for justice is the balance. An equitable outcome is one where both sides are balanced.

At best, it could be said that our leadership appears to be unbalanced. This is not just at a local level but at the highest levels on the world stage. Leaders are not jailed for criminality, nor are there seemingly any sanctions for poor performance. No bankers have gone to jail for their role in the 2009 crisis. Most of the banks have just taken up where they left off.

This, in itself, is strange. Our political leaders must realize they are aided and abetted by a new communications environment, which favours the sensationalist over the modest, the loud over the quiet and the liar over the truth teller. Why would they not want those who caused so much hardship to undergo public censure? Perhaps because it would take too long to punish? Perhaps because it would certainly not rehabilitate? Perhaps because the long-term economic benefits of the Faustian pact outweigh any short-term political gain?

The bankers absolved themselves by describing the credit crisis as 'a credit tsunami',[63] almost as if it were an act of God, something beyond their control. What is the point of a central banking system unless someone is in charge of global economic flows? Can this be put down to a lack of imagination? The facts were there. Inverted yield curves and mortgage defaults. Some entrepreneurial sorts interpreted them correctly.[64] Perhaps, as Upton Sinclair said, 'It is difficult to get a man to understand something, when his salary depends upon his not understanding it.'[65]

Some might argue that the best way of testing the morality of a system is to subject it to countervailing behaviour and see whether it rights itself. Alexis De Tocqueville[66] would be pleased to see his work still being discussed and tested 150 years after he wrote it.

This might be of academic interest, were it not for the profound effects of leadership failure on every aspect of our life, including political mandates and parliamentary democracies. When world tensions are rising and political experience is lacking, the timing for this failure could not be worse.

The way we teach leadership – an overemphasis on individuality and specialism

Our schools and universities have become ever more obsessed with grades. There's a right answer. It's at the back of the book. Those who can deduce the right answer. Those who can analyse. Those who can drill down. These are the winners. These are the ones that are elevated. It drives us towards leaders who are quantitative, short-term, tactical, tangible and cold. We taught people to think, not to feel. An inability to join the dots. Leaders must cope with ambiguity. It's better to know a little about many things rather than a lot about a few things. The age of the specialist leader is dead. There are now so many criteria for the leader to consider from a wide range of sources. Fortunately, this is more available than ever before with the advent of big data. The leader needs a broad situational fluency to understand what's happening.

But most of us have been trained as specialists. The education system and the institutional taxonomies require labels – the person is an accountant, lawyer, technician, scientist or salesperson. It's quite exciting to find someone who has two seemingly unconnected skills, like a scientist who can do sales. This focus on drilling down into ever more specialist skill sets prevents the development of polymaths. It certainly creates the comfortable intellectual certainties of identity. It allows us to pigeonhole and put someone in a box or class. The problem with this desire for certainty is that it positions outliers – both top and bottom – for attention. Ranking the class on any one specialism enhances the egos of those at both the top and the bottom. It makes them both outliers. The good ones become good, the bad ones revel in their badness. In Malcolm Gladwell's *Outliers*,[67] he explains how birthdates, for instance, make a huge difference in how excellence develops. He points out that those born towards the beginning of the school year exhibit the best talent, when in reality they are simply almost a year older than the youngest in the class. At school, this makes a huge difference and sets a pattern that is difficult to break later in life.

Again, the imbalance is clearly visible. The worth of a student is in how many right answers they can achieve, not in how they help a fellow student. No one sees the bigger picture. There are few 'marks', if any, for those who collaborate with others. In fact, these days collaboration is more often termed plagiarism and penalized.

Too many incompetent men – a lack of balanced skills

The system is designed to make us think in terms of winners and losers. There can only be one winner. This is inherently wrong. It reflects an inherently male bias in education and measurability. We give no marks for collaboration, sensitivity, empathy, humility. Individualistic assessment favours the competitive. This helps explain the bias against women in science and maths.

This approach is instilled at the earliest stages in the education system and is linked to reckless risk taking and short-termism. Such training is antithetical to the best interests of the entire community. As leaders have gained less tenure, they have to do more in ever shorter periods of time. The overwhelming need 'to do' rather than 'be' or have values emerges.

The traditional model of the infallible gifted leader has its roots in the Judeo-Christian focus on Moses and Christ. This is a male model. The Arthurian legend is similar. Think of Alexander, Caesar, Napoleon, the Pope and Martin Luther King. It's the father figure, but laced with overconfidence and unrealistic expectations. When we think about leadership, the focus is always on the leader and not the 'ship'. The focus on one person automatically implies a lack of teamwork. Where leadership fails, there's been a breakdown in responsibility.

Overconfidence as a source of narrow thinking

There is something else here. Could the imbalance be manifesting as reckless overconfidence? In an interview in 2013 for the *Harvard Business Review*, Professor Tomas Chamorro-Premuzic, from University College London (UCL), talked about how too much confidence can mask incompetence.[68] He said that:

> … confident people tend to be more charismatic, extroverted, and socially skilled, which in most cultures are highly desirable features… in virtually every culture, confidence is equated with competence.

So, we automatically assume that confident people are also more skilled or talented. Or put another way, we assume unbalanced people are balanced. Chamorro-Premuzic points out that:

> Competent people are generally confident, but confident people are not generally competent. They're good at hiding incompetence and insecurities… mostly because they are self-deceived themselves, so they generally think that they are much better than they actually are.

He points out that the problem with overconfidence begins with an unbalanced recruitment and interview process. This is not set up to establish competence, usually because the many leadership skills are difficult to assess independently. Assessing candidate competence is an objective of the process, but confidence is so often the method or the path taken to assess it. That route leads to inaccurate evaluations of people's competence. So, for example, most people who interview really well and are assumed to be great are in reality just charming the interviewers during that

session. Chamorro-Premuzic says that people need to understand that the main goal of interviewing is to discover competency.
Interviewers shouldn't really care about the confidence of candi-
dates. Perhaps it just represents our desperate desire to believe
that there is a leader that conforms to the historic legacy models
we've inherited?

Humility is perhaps a better indicator of competence because
it operates as a reality check and it helps maintain awareness of
weaknesses. This drives self-improvement as well. All of the
evidence from psychological research suggests humility makes
leaders more likeable. The conclusion is that when people
perceive leadership as more competent than it thinks it is, the
more it likes it.

Imagine a world where doctors, teachers, engineers or pilots
are selected on the basis of their confidence, as opposed to their
actual ability. Until we stop appointing leaders on the basis of
their confidence rather than competence, we will keep having
balance problems.

Chamorro-Premuzic believes this will also keep making it
hard for women, who are usually both humbler and more competent than men in these domains. As far as the gender debate is
concerned, he says the problem is not that women lack confidence. It's rather that men have too much of it.

He also says the criteria we use to evaluate men are different
from those used to evaluate women. He points out that when
men come across as confident or even arrogant, we assume that
they are good at what they do and we call them charismatic.
When women behave in the same way:

> ... we tend to see them as psychopathic or a threat to society or
> an organisation. So, society punishes manifestations of confidence
> in women, and rewards them in men – which only reinforces this
> natural difference between the genders.

He says the main reason for the imbalanced management sex ratio is our inability to discern between confidence and competence. If that's the case, then it conveniently absolves men alone as the cause.

This makes sense, but what if the leadership environment has become so attuned to analytical thinking that it's become associated exclusively with masculine thought-process thinking? Could it be that men think that because they're more short-term, data-driven, they're much smarter than women? Arrogance and overconfidence are inversely related to leadership talent. Much of leadership ability is about building and maintaining high-performing teams where followers set aside their personal agendas to work for the common interest of the group.

One conclusion from Chamorro-Premuzic's work might be that masculine thinking alone can be the cause of imbalance. It leads to more analytic, more short-term, tactical, arrogant, manipulative, risk-prone and divisive thinking.

Communication, yes, but no conversation – no balance of human processes

As Alex Beard puts it in *Natural Born Learners: Our incredible capacity to learn and how we can harness it*:[69]

> Our era demands more of our human talents – empathy, creativity, sociability – and raises the spectre of a future in which we'll need others, like drive, determination and resilience. We're living under the shadow of an epidemic of mental problems. In 2016, one in seven 16- to 24-year-olds in the UK experienced mental illness (anxiety, depression and panic disorder, phobia or obsessive-compulsive disorder). The World Health Organization estimates that 450 million people are currently affected by mental disorders globally that one in four will suffer at some point in their lives. Strength of character is now needed to stay sane, let alone thrive.

Paul Barnwell, a high-school teacher in the US, wrote in *The Atlantic:*[70] 'I came to realize that conversational competence might be the single-most overlooked skill we fail to teach students.' No conversation means no negotiation. No ability to negotiate. No ability to solve emotional problems. No ability to hear the other person's point of view.

This is perhaps the greatest problem for the next generation of leaders. They don't know how to listen or how to converse. Calvin Coolidge said, 'No man ever listened himself out of a job.'[71] If they don't know how to listen, they can't hold a conversation and they can't lead. Face-to-face conversations matter. People cannot read you well enough with emojis. Nor can you read them.

In the great volume of communication from outside, we've become uninterested or too distracted to read the subtle signs of human behaviour among those closest to us. This has caused a lack of balance between the reception of distanced signals to those proximate.

The essence of this argument was put forward by Avner Offer, Emeritus Professor of Economics at All Souls College, Oxford: 'The flow of novelty is so strong that higher levels of commitment and self-discipline are needed to ensure that long-term well-being is not sacrificed for short-term gratification.'[72] These are qualities other than those recognized by the standard curriculum as illustrated by Alex Beard,[73] writing about the Knowledge is Power Program (KIPP) in the US. This has been written on the wall of every classroom: Self-control, Grit, Optimism, Social Intelligence, Gratitude, Curiosity and Zest. This may be pointing to a world where character point average becomes as important as grade point average.

There is also another issue here. We haven't yet explained how girls can be ahead of boys at almost every level in school yet fall behind men later in the workplace in terms of leadership and salary achievements. Could it be that there is an inherent bias against women in the adult world, that does not apply to girls? We'll investigate this in more depth later.

Lost in the fog

It is not just one element as above that has become imbalanced. If that were so, it could be easily corrected. The challenge here is that so many of the balance axes have been upended.

In the last 25 years, the world's leadership culture has shifted on its axis. It used to be an overwhelmingly male, heterosexual, patient, predictable, factual, planned, white, long-term, Western-orientated, technology-leveraged, deflationary, structured, left-brained rational, broadcast, top-down, militarily symmetric world.

Now, leadership is operating in an inverted, unreal, amoral, impatient, inflationary, selfish, spiritual, irrational, gender-fluid, polysexual, strategically multipolar, everywhere-facing, bottom-up, information-soaked, multiracial, androgynous, fluid, opinion-ated, rapidly moving, asymmetric world.

Our leaders are completely unprepared for this kind of leadership. Many get to the top through a specialism and by studying management or business. Neither of these is about leadership and none of these educational courses is conducted under conditions of rapid change. Management courses are a series of static storyboards. Leadership is a live movie.

In an age of information overload and over-stimulus, we have to face the possibility that facts are dull. And we don't want our news to be full of dull facts. Therefore, an industry has grown up around confecting stories and it is not a new one. It has been going on since Julius Caesar reported the Gallic Wars. The difference now is the scale and the automation.

The biggest lesson here is that abundance leads to contempt, waste and misuse. It is true of any natural resource. It is certainly true of information. Leaders in this environment still need to have a narrative (constructed out of information) and this needs to compete with other narratives (possibly constructed out of disin-formation). The problem is that the recipients, thus confronted with often multiple complex narratives, are unable to differentiate. They choose either the easiest to understand, the most frequently repeated or the most attractively presented, or even better, all three.

Not only is this the case but opinion is also much easier to circulate. Here, ancient rules still apply – the empty vessels make the loudest noises. This leaves the individual with a trust problem as opinion may not be fact but is still a consideration.

Leaders when subjected to scrutiny are weakened by the crime of 'I don't know', 'I'm not sure' or 'It doesn't feel right'. When confronted with scepticism, they're forced to up their level of certainty. It's a natural reaction. This then leads to pinning their colours to the mast and consequently going down with the ship (to extend the naval metaphor).

The lack of qualitative measures

Perhaps the largest aspect of how we assess leadership is in the measurement we use. Successful leaders are most often measured on the size, scale and dominance of the business. Of course, success with customers and colleagues is important but this is assumed by financial success. The examples of successful leadership are always about those who have experienced success, rather than those with a *successful attitude*. The latter is a surer indicator of long-term success than one-off achievement.

In Daniel Pink's book *Drive: The surprising truth about what motivates us*,[74] he relates that those who won silver medals before gold medals at the Olympics were more likely to go on to consistent gold medal success. The reason for this being that the pain of being first loser was enough to motivate them to win next time. The Olympic model and motto are all about individual superlative – *Citius, Altius, Fortius* (Faster, Higher, Stronger). This is measurement in the physical realm.

We have no convincing ways of measuring happiness, fairness, collaboration or belief in the organization. Nonetheless, these are all signs of leadership. Neither do we have ways of measuring group collaboration, say, for instance as in an orchestra. We can measure aptitude but seemingly not happiness.

In Matthew Crawford's book about jobs that involve working manually, he raised some interesting points about shop craft as it is called in the US.[75] He highlights that as a person who was also academically gifted, working with his hands, being a motorcycle engine enthusiast, the system somehow saw him as a failure. But this is to say that academic achievement was seen as the only legitimate course for 'success'. To see it as such is a spiritual failure on a massive level. How has it come to this? Of course, Crawford has the right to do what he wants. He relates that he just enjoyed fixing things. Somehow, in the course of becoming educated, it seems that his personal choice of what to do with his life was ignored, not valued.

The lack of role models

How can it be then that losers are also winners? Could it be that the normative behaviours established by schools first then universities later are warped? Could it be that they establish the criteria for success based upon their own experience of 'success'? This normative field then establishes a square-peg mentality that says that all round pegs need to be hammered into these holes.

Schools are powerful agents of the 'there is only one right answer and it's at the back of the book' school of thought. This does not prepare anyone for the myriad paradoxes that leadership is presented with. Academic achievement versus happiness? To want your education to prepare you for being happy is not a goal that is written into many educational curricula.

Why doesn't this ever change? It is very hard to fight a school. You will find teachers, students and other parents against you for one good reason. If you want to change the system in favour of finding the future that is likely to make your child happy, then you will be attacked. Very likely the provenance of this attack will be the basis that your child cannot hack it intellectually and therefore is not a success. And round we go.

'My child must experience what I experienced' is also a powerful force acting against change. 'I have a degree therefore you will have a degree to give you the skills required to cope with life.' It sounds like life is something to be endured. Hardly a good model for creating happy teams.

Furthermore, could it also be that schools often work to a national agenda, established by other 'anywhere'[76] thinkers? If some do not want to 'go away' to university, does this not make them locals? Again, could it be that staying somewhere rather aspiring to be anywhere is tantamount to failure?

Philosophy as a destination, not a vehicle

It's become a curious phenomenon that universities have become a place for the study of philosophy rather than the practice of it. The age of data has given us more to analyse and measure. We've been taught to distrust anything that is nuanced or ambiguous. For instance, the implications and understanding of St Augustine's ideas that there is inside each of us a 'God-shaped hole'. He pointed out that at the heart of some of the most ambitious, driven and successful leaders is a place that no amount of wealth, recognition and status can fill. His message was that if we try to put anything else in there, it won't fit because it won't meet the spiritual need we have inside of our heart/soul.

We've created education systems where there are only right answers. Where thinking triumphs over feeling.

We've thus created education systems where there are only right answers. Where thinking triumphs over feeling. Where thinking is clarity and feelings are not to be trusted. Where speed is highly valued as efficiency, and qualities such as patience designated the realm of the 'loser'. Where financial success is more valued than any other aspect of leadership. Where national and global thinking is promoted at the expense of the local and parochial (even the word is most usually pejorative). Everything and everyone is measured and graded and yet strangely happiness has become entirely secondary.

Summary

We have seen leadership failures in just about every part of our lives. Scandals have been recorded in churches, charities, entertainment, politics and commerce. The leadership failure caused the financial crash of 2007–2009 and this hugely impacted our economy. Why did it happen when our leaders were educated, experienced and academically qualified? They were surrounded by data sources. It was, in the accepted sense, qualified in every respect, yet it still failed. It points clearly to a fault in our education and preparation for leadership. These leaders had education but no imagination.

The failures caused a decade of harm and the wrongdoers went largely unpunished. The financial costs alone were $22 trillion. The cost emotionally and spiritually was even greater. It provoked a lot of anger, which undermined trust in all leadership further and continues to do so today.

The common denominator in the failures was a profound imbalance that manifested itself as unethical behaviour in the form of greed, short-termism and reckless overconfidence, especially among middle-aged, experienced, qualified men. It is ironic that such supreme overconfidence in a small number should have resulted in an enduring lack of confidence and sense of insecurity in so many others.

Although we can see this problem clearly in hindsight ten years on, these are not at all new problems. The story of mankind's struggle with balance is what our heritage, culture and history are all about. Next, we zoom out to look at that and explore the concept of the infinite challenge to remain balanced at the zero point on the positive and negative scales.

CHAPTER TWO

Circles and zeros

What is the history of balance? What significance does the concept of zero have? What imagery and symbolism are passed down to us from history? Is there a role for a greater spiritualism that connects leadership and love? Do qualitative assessments matter? How does this differ around the world?

We come into this world with nothing and we leave with nothing. Our life is parenthesized by zeros. Zero is also a symbol. Most of the religious texts tell us this. We've known about the concept of zero since the Sumerians in Mesopotamian culture. We have real difficulty, however, with things that have double meanings. This is because we've been trained to look at the world analytically and mathematically. So, when we see a zero, we think null, valueless, nothing. But if we go back in history, we see many symbols of zero that keep a deeper meaning alive.

A circle, a zero can be infinite and encompass everything. Love is also infinite and all-encompassing. Euclid's first common notion is that things that are equal to the same thing are equal to each other. If a zero can be infinite and all-encompassing and so is love, then the zero is also love – a state of infinite possibility.

What's love got to do with it?

Love is a word that is guaranteed to cause sweat to break out in a boardroom or a cabinet meeting. What's love got to do with it? Our answer is: everything. We can track some of our leadership problems to the fact love is not being brought to work. Leaders who act from a point of selfishness, who do not have the interests of others in mind, are not acting from a place of love. Without love for others, it is hard to transcend from a zero to the start of unlimited possibility.

If only we could find the formula, we too could transform nothing into something really big and really valuable. If the definition of magic[1] is 'the power of apparently influencing events by using mysterious or supernatural forces' then we are going to argue that mysterious forces do exist that can transform today's nightmares into tomorrow's dreams.

Love is a word that is guaranteed to cause sweat to break out in a boardroom or a cabinet meeting.

After all, how did Martin Luther King transform US society? He said, 'I have a dream.' How did Gandhi transform India into an independent nation? He said, 'In a gentle way you can shake the world.' The mysterious force here is love – love of others, not love of leadership for its own sake. This is why these ideas have magic in them. They contain the ineffable but immediately understandable nature of the human condition.

Magic

We are frequently anxious and sceptical when removed from the logical and the familiar. These days, we're more comfortable with calling our magic something else. We ask, what is the 'secret sauce' that makes a company or a country perform better than others? Somehow, we are more comfortable with the idea that there is a magic secret recipe, like the recipe for Coca-Cola or the recipe for the sauce on a Big Mac or the 'Happiness Index' that the nation of Bhutan developed. We want to quantify love and magic and load it with logic. But it is hard to capture with tools of analysis.

Still, we know that very successful leadership models can be based on love. Witness the undisputed success of New Zealand's famed All Blacks who have dominated the game of rugby globally for decades. Their leadership model is based on love of the team members. They are always treated as if they were family. The All Blacks place their faith in the love of the team symbols like the jersey, which they always strive to 'leave in a better place', and the Haka dance, which serves to honour the tribe's pride, unity and ancestral history. Military leaders consistently say that their leadership models are always based on love. To become a Navy SEAL, it is not enough to survive the physical rigours of training and 'Hell Week'.[2] A person must also display the commitment to risk one's own life to save the life of a fellow SEAL. Love of another's life must exceed love for your own. And yet even this is not enough. One can succeed by putting love of the team or community ahead of one's own interests. One former Navy SEAL wrote a book in which he explained why love is the magic ingredient that causes a candidate to become a SEAL:[3]

> Even in great pain, faced with the test of their lives, they had the ability to step-outside their own pain, put aside their own fear and ask: How can I help the guy next to me? They had more than the 'fist' of courage and physical strength. They also had a heart large enough to think about others, to dedicate themselves to a higher purpose.

Yet the writer, former SEAL Eric Greitens, ended up having to resign as the Governor of Missouri when a sex scandal threatened him with impeachment. Was he considering the needs of the state or of his constituents or of the person he allegedly assaulted? Was he capable of putting another person's needs or a community's needs ahead of his own? Yes. But why didn't he? A loss of balance? That is the leadership question we are all grappling with now and it is an ancient problem.

The idea we're describing rests at the core of many religions. Let's take Buddhism for instance. Buddha was born as Siddhārtha Gautama, the son of a regional Indian king 500 years before Christ. Although he was wealthy, he renounced possessions in favour of religious study. He had to strip himself of things until he had nothing to become master of 'zero'. His core belief was based on never being allowed to argue or try to persuade others by opposing, criticizing, coaxing, denying or disputing. The Buddhist belief is that nothing in this world is absolute. There is no right or wrong, good or bad, or left or right on any subject. Everything is full of potential. Many entrepreneurial leaders will be familiar with this approach to situations, places and people alike. This is essentially the 'magic' of leadership.

Why do we need to think about this? It is because our leadership class keeps assuming the world is a zero-sum game. In their effort to win elections, to outperform in stock markets, to command outcomes in communities, they are consistently falling into ethical lapses and tragic behaviours. The bad leadership we see is so pervasive, any one leader's story cannot adequately explain the problem. It is not just about how Harvey Weinstein behaved or that the management at Volkswagen should have come clean on emissions instead of lying to the public or that the Catholic Church should not have tried to cover up sexual abuse. The problem is systemic. It cuts across all categories of leadership, all institutions, all cultures and all geographical locations. The problem is our modern obsession with the idea that there is a perfect and infallible leader, if only we could find them. The problem is that our leaders are not thinking holistically about

The problem is our modern obsession with the idea that there is a perfect and infallible leader, if only we could find them.

their role in society. Instead of viewing the world as a dog-eat-dog, zero-sum world where winning by any means is worth it, we need our leaders to see that zero leadership would serve us better. That doesn't mean no leadership. It means a leadership that balances between positives and negatives, between competing forces, between conflicting objectives and interests. This is what we have called the 'Infinite Leader'.

The concept of *nothing* originated in Eastern Asia and is expressed using the character 空 (Kuu) in Japanese which means 'sky', 'void' or 'emptiness'. The mathematical zero was first developed in India around 650 AD. It was conceived as a way of representing 'nothingness' for complex calculations, but the original sign for zero was also known as 'sunya' – a concept from Indian philosophy to describe 'emptiness', 'void' or 'sky'. So, there was a similarity in these early concepts. Zero emerged in India as a Bindu, a circle with a dot inside. It arose from a state of mind in yogic practice. It was the point at which the mind transcends everything and all experiences collapse into a universal one. The zero with a dot is considered the point from which all things emerged. It is a place of endless and unlimited possibility. Zero stands as a mirror image to infinity. After all, if you divide zero by zero by zero, you still get zero and this goes on for infinity.

Zero is transcendent. An infinite. It is neither thinking nor doing. It is perfectly *in balance*. It is, quite literally, nothing and everything. A zero is not just a number. It is a symbol that represents the start of possibility. We will argue that we will get better leaders and a better society if we can learn to create something out of nothing. Our leaders will not do this alone. Each one of us, the person who is just trying to get by or the one trying to get ahead, has a part to play in creating the conditions for a superior society. Leadership does not happen alone. We are all part of the leadership process and have a part to play in the leadership we are getting. Given that modern leadership is continuously experiencing crises in virtually every sector of the economy and every quarter of society, something needs to change. We need to make a leap into a different way of being leaders and a different way of choosing those who lead us.

Zero is not just a number. It is also an ancient symbol of infinite possibility. Zero is the sister to infinity. The zero point is the target. The Infinite Leader is the one who leads with the greatest balance and who creates the conditions to transcend limitations. The Infinite Leader sees the possible where all others see the impossible. The best leaders have always done this.

Circles

Geometric shapes have been part of human religious symbolism for thousands of years, long before they became mathematical symbols used by the Egyptians and Greeks. Pythagoras believed that geometry was the rational understanding of God, man and nature.

Circles are among the oldest of symbols and commonly represent unity, wholeness and infinity. Pythagoras called the circle 'monad'; this refers, in cosmogony, to the supreme being, divinity or the totality of all things. In the Zen Buddhist philosophy, a circle stands for enlightenment and perfection in unity with the primal principles. Circles are sometimes symbols of the Judeo-Christian God and sanctity, appearing as halos. Circles are also often seen as protective symbols. In occult practices, standing within a circle shields people from supernatural dangers or outside influences, ie a magic circle. Leaders have an 'inner circle'.

In the *Dictionary of Symbolism*[4] by Allison Protas, Geoff Brown, Jamie Smith and Eric Jaffe at the University of Michigan,[5] the circle is:

A universal symbol with extensive meaning. It represents the notions of totality, wholeness, original perfection, the Self, the infinite, eternity, timelessness, all cyclic movement, God. As the sun, it is masculine power; as the soul and as encircling waters, it is the feminine maternal principle. It implies an idea of movement, and symbolizes the cycle of time, the perpetual motion of everything that moves, the planets' journey around the sun (the circle of the zodiac), the great rhythm of the universe.

A zero is a circular symbol. As Manuel Lima vividly describes in his *Book of Circles*,[6] throughout history a circle has stood for 'unity and wholeness, for movement and cyclicality and for eternity and perpetuity'. It is a sign of simplicity, perfection and balance. We have built powerful structures and ideas around the circle as an organizing principle.

When we divide this circle-based symbol, we see yin and yang, which represent balance (Figure 2.1).

When we begin to double this circular symbol, we see the start of many conceptual tools we have relied upon throughout time. Two overlapping circles give us Venn diagrams.

It is no accident that so many successful brand logos are built within a circle because these symbolize trust. Buildings based on circles convey this same message of infinity and trust.

In a *Fast Company* piece entitled 'Why the shape of a company's logo matters',[7] Annie Sneed investigated the shapes of logos. Shapes have important resonances. The first shape a baby sees is the roundness of its mother's eyes. Research has shown that consumers like a brand more, the more they look at the logo. Given these past findings, Professor of Marketing at INSEAD Amitava Chattopadhyay thought something as simple as a logo's

FIGURE 2.1 Yin and yang

overall shape might change the way people felt about companies. He says that people associate circular shapes with soft, comfy things and angular shapes with hard, sturdy things:

> If you think about it, circular shapes on average tend to be quite soft – balls, pillows, mattresses – whereas angular shapes like bricks, tables, and knives tend to be hard and durable. These associations probably form over time because that's how we encounter the world.[8]

Some research seems to indicate that consumers perceive shoes with a circular logo as more comfortable. Other research shows that airlines with circular logos are perceived as more sensitive towards customers. Circular logos portray security, continuity and protection.

Think of the Oval Office. Think of the round chambers of so many parliaments. Think of round churches. Think of iconic modern buildings like Apple's headquarters, which is called the Ring, and the headquarters of the British intelligence agency, GCHQ, which is called the Doughnut. Think of the Millennium Wheel, the giant ferris wheel located on London's South Bank. Think of the Holy Trinity, a mandala (which means circle in Sanskrit), targets, Roman arenas, Greek temples, the planet itself (and its rotation), sports stadia and the ring in Tolkien stories. These are all based on the symbol of a circle that we usually reduce analytically to a numerical zero, failing to recognize the inherent power of a circle. A circle produces rotation and is thus a powerful symbol of generative force. One person sees a zero and another sees timeless symbolism of the circle of life like the ouroboros. This is a serpent eating its own tail as it sheds its ego and transforms itself into something new. Others see the Wheel of Dharma, which represents the ability to hold all of Buddha's teachings together. It is the ensō image that represents the Zen state. The implication of the zero concept was so profound that the Buddhists dedicated themselves to following its principle.

The qualities of a circle

The zero, being a circle, conveys many qualities. The famed art critic Ruskin explained that a circle in the world of art inevitably stands for six things: unity, infinity, repose, symmetry, purity and moderation. A circle is the basis of stability for ancient and modern alike – Greek temples and more contemporary structures, such as Buckminster Fuller's buckyballs, or fullerenes. Buckyballs are composed of carbon atoms linked to other carbon atoms by covalent bonds, in the same pattern of hexagons and pentagons you find on a soccer ball, giving the same spherical structures known to ancient Greeks.

We base our guiding tools on this symbol. Think of sundials, compasses, astrolabes, globes, zodiacs, notions of the cycle of time and even Mercator maps, which are all based on round configurations. The zero is a bullseye and the start of every single thing that spirals from nothing into something.

Pi, the universal constant, the golden ratio, is nothing more than the ratio of a circle's circumference to its diameter. It underpins the structure of everything in the universe.

You can think of zero as the balancing point or the origin of a graph. Zero need not be at the bottom left of a graph. It might be in the centre, as it is with Cartesian coordinates. Zero then becomes a pivotal number between being and not being. It becomes infinite.

Zero as the devil

The whole concept of zero has caused a great deal of problems for theologists and philosophers alike. In Genesis, the Bible says:

> In the beginning God created the heaven and the earth. And the earth was without form, and void; and darkness was upon the face of the deep. And the Spirit of God moved upon the face of

the waters. And God said, Let there be light: and there was light. And God saw the light, that it was good: and God divided the light from the darkness.

The implicit suggestion is that before God showed up, there was nothing and this is, of course, infinite. This is why Judeo-Christian philosophy had such a problem with the concept of zero. It was synonymous with the devil, or absence of everything including God. It was also shunned arithmetically by the Greeks because they used their calculations (from calculus meaning pebble – used in the early abacus) to measure land or area. There was no such thing as negative space, so they excluded it.

What does all this have to do with leadership? Today we make most of our leadership choices based on historical faith and culture. In the West, this is still mainly a Judeo-Christian model. Christianity gives us a false belief that one person, usually a man, has all the answers. Whether it's Jesus Christ or Steve Jobs, Moses or Elon Musk. Further back the words we use for leader share the same etymology, eg Shah, Czar and Kaiser, all stem from the Latin word 'Caesar' – an all-conquering hero.

In China, Japan, parts of Asia, Africa and across the Middle East we still believe that the world works best when there is one person in charge. It is commonplace these days to hear people admire the 'strong-man' approach. Many believe that democracies can't succeed as well as more centralized and authoritarian regimes. This is because we still follow the single infallible person and believe that they will be the universal panacea to all our woes. We follow them despite their weaknesses. In fact, we may follow them *because* of their weaknesses. We buy the bravado and promote whoever speaks loudest and first. Writing for *Psychology Today*, Gregg Murray[9] points out the research still shows that we like leaders who are physically tall, big and loud. It may be that all this has something to do with the way we keep ending up with people in leadership positions who are prone to ethical lapses and bad judgement.

The leadership crises of recent years have occurred in almost every quarter of society from corporations to churches to community leaders. Trust in institutions and leadership has suffered greatly. We are now in a societal crisis because of the extraordinary belief that there is a Superman and the loss of faith as we keep being shown that he does not exist. It has to do with the way we are choosing our leaders. It has to do with the way our leaders are coming into power with their own interests in mind and without much regard for the consequences of their actions on others.

Leadership affects everything. Every person, every organization, every sports team, every political system, every religion, every orchestra, every community, every family has a leader. It is everywhere around us. Yet never has it appeared to be so discredited. Why is this? Why have our leaders lost sight of us, those who follow them? Why do so few of us experience leadership at first hand? What has changed in our world that makes leadership so rare and highly sought after? What is leadership and why is it seen as the preserve of the few, not the many? Do those at the top fear for their positions? Is this why they don't teach it? Is it because our current leaders behave as if they are entitled to lead? If so, then that's not leadership.

When we do teach leadership, why do we confuse it with business management?

Why do we not teach leadership in our schools? Are we too busy teaching that there are only right and wrong answers? When we do teach leadership, why do we confuse it with business management? Are they the same things? Why are we constantly analysing and measuring every aspect of our work? Why do we distrust happiness and contentment? Is it because they can't be measured? The profundity of skill or education does not dictate leadership, nor do core competencies alone. If this were the case, then every orchestra would be led by the best soloist.

Summary

For centuries, the notion of balance and the pursuit of it has been central to human thinking. It has been at the heart of our organized religion and culture. It has been seen as a goal that will deliver wisdom and sustainability. Just because organized religion has become less important to leadership thinking, it doesn't mean we should throw away some of its most important teachings.

The symbolism associated with balance is frequently that of circles, possibly because it is a naturally occurring shape. For example, the shape of our mother's iris. It has been described as presenting unity, infinity, repose, symmetry, purity and moderation. This is why family brand logo marks are often circular. Zero is also circular and has been used in many civilizations to represent infinity or balance. For example, the *yin* and *yang* image. It's also been used to represent the devil.

It's clear that we've known for centuries that balance is important and the history of mankind has been the pursuit of balance. This can be seen in the struggles between faith and science, or tradition and modernity. However we look at it, the idea of balance is important. Next, we look at our pursuit of greater efficiency in leadership and the analytic, scientific, reductionist techniques that we have applied. This is not a balanced approach at all. It's a new type of imbalance, as we shall see.

CHAPTER THREE

Existing leadership models

How have traditional leadership models contributed to the imbalance? How has the pursuit of efficiency changed our understanding of the leadership task? Can balance be better calibrated? Does it happen automatically? How can we use our understanding to achieve better balance?

We said in *The Leadership Lab* that we believed the only true provenance of certainty must be mediocrity. It turns out that, like all ideas, this is not wholly original. Not for the first time, Descartes got there first:

> If you would be a real seeker after truth, it is necessary that at least once in your life you doubt, as far as possible, all things. Doubt is the origin of wisdom.

There were a large number of ironies and dualities in the life of René Descartes, a Frenchman who lived much of his life in the Netherlands. He was a mathematician and philosopher. He is best known for 'I think, therefore I am' (*cogito ergo sum*) and for coming up with the Cartesian coordinates on which our models are based. The full quotation includes the word 'dubito' in front of 'cogito ergo sum', which means I doubt, therefore I think, therefore I am. Descartes' point was that the act of doubting one's own existence served as proof of the reality of one's own mind, which must be thinking and therefore must be present, and therefore real. It also points to humility, a key leadership quality.

Not so rational

This leader of rationality had an emotional and irrational side to his personal life. This is often the case. One extreme capability of the mind is homeostatically defended against the other. The further the travel in one direction, the more the response in the other. This is illustrated by a curious story. In 1635, Descartes had a daughter named Francine with Hélène Jans who was one of his servants. He defied the morals of the era and lived with them both. Francine contracted scarlet fever and died at the age of five. Grieving, Descartes consoled himself by building a mechanical automaton replica of the child. The wind-up mechanical doll 'slept' in a casket next to his bed and travelled with him everywhere. He spent years perfecting his skills as a clockmaker and a constructor of mechanical toys. His work on early automatons is now studied by experts on robotics and AI. This early mechanical bot stayed by his side for many years until 1646 when Queen Christina of Sweden sent for him to discuss something the rationalist thinker clearly had strong views about, namely 'love, hatred, and the passions of the soul'.[1] During the journey the ship's crew were overcome with curiosity and stumbled upon the fake child. They were so frightened by her lifelike qualities that they threw her overboard and accused Descartes of witchcraft. Remember this was a time of witchcraft trials. Descartes was so overcome with grief at the loss of the doll that he died only six months later. It just goes to show that even the most famed rationalist had an emotional side, a spiritual aspect to his personality and a deep longing for the physical presence of a deceased loved one.

The importance of zero

Descartes exemplified both a rational and an emotional life. But we forget his pained emotional life. Instead, what we laud him for is his rational thought process. We take his philosophy to mean, if I'm not thinking, then I don't exist. By default then, it's difficult to prove that anything else exists. This is to say that there is no such thing as the void or 'zero' because it cannot be verified by man, therefore we cannot be sure it actually exists.

His Cartesian coordinates, though, accept the existence of zero as the origin through which both his axes pass as a nominal fulcrum. When Descartes developed this model, it was a break-through. Suddenly shapes could become graphs.[2] His ideas permitted a marriage that had many consequences. The Pythagorean Greek models of geometry and their measurement of space could now be joined with the Arabic model of algebra. This is an Arabic word literally meaning a 'reunion of broken parts'. The significance of algebra's relationship with zero cannot be overstated. Algebra allows us to find the unknown, so if:

$$2x + 1 = 5$$

then we can deduce that $x = 2$. 'x' is, of course, an unknown. But then so was zero in the Greek tradition. The Greeks had no use for it. Their mathematics was largely based around geometry – literally the measurement of the earth. The concept of negative anything was alien and illogical.

The metaphor here though is compelling. When we're looking for real leadership, many people refer to an 'x' factor. Something that is mysterious, intangible and qualitative. Of course, as soon as we venture into this realm, we're going to excite the critical faculties of the university-trained, left-brained approach.... .

Let's try though. There's a wealth of mystery around us, but we live with it just the same. We even accept its importance. Take love for instance. You could study love. You could analyse it. You could read every book that's ever been written about it. You could write a thesis on it. But if you've never experienced it, how could you ever understand it?

Take the two approaches side by side. The critical mind would ask: How can you tell you're in love? What are the signs? Are there symptoms? Does your heart beat faster? Are your mental faculties degraded? Can other people tell? How do they know? When did they know? What happened? Who falls in love? Why?

But anyone who's been in love knows different. If you're really in love, you don't ask such questions. Love is not rational. It does not follow a Western reductionist academic model. Love is not judgemental. Love does not divide or analyse. Love doesn't 'drill down', it looks across. You can't solve it with a theorem. You can't prove it in court. You don't get to choose who you fall in love with. Or where that happens. Or when. Those who go in search of love seldom find it. You can't find it. Love finds you. We all like to think we're in control of our lives, but we're not. You can't plan it. You can't ordain it. Love is not a choice. If you're asking rational questions, then I'm sorry, you're not in love. If you're truly in love, you're only capable of making vowel sounds, but you can say at least that you understand it.

From a scientific point of view, the link between Cartesian coordinates and algebra was heady stuff. The slope of a line is the change that occurs in its height either in the horizontal or the vertical plane. This can be represented as Δx horizontally or Δy vertically. Thus was born the child of this marriage – and the tormentor of many an adolescent – differential calculus. This from a military point of view has massive implications. It was used in Newtonian physics, atomic theory and the space programme.

Fortunately, we have no need of anything quite so complex in our models.

Zero as a fulcrum

In the Cartesian sense, zero can be interpreted in another way. It is no longer nothing but representative of a fulcrum, a pivot around which a scale can be applied. This is zero as neutral, disinterested or unbiased. We're not saying leadership should be this alone, only that it should at least be capable of it. Leaders are supposed to be passionate and committed, but they are also required to be fair and balanced.

Leaders are supposed to be passionate and committed, but they are also required to be fair and balanced.

One person's fair and balanced might be another's extreme. So, what are we really talking about here? We're saying the leader should strive to be the most flexible member of the team. This means they can be cheerleader in chief at the same time as being drill-down analyst. They can be orientated to individual objectives while at the same time being group-focused.

This gives us the possibility that real leadership can be superpositioned between extremes on a continuum. This is not to say they would be highly volatile, just capable of using their judgement to articulate the polarities while also able to return to balance. Think of this as an elastic web, where the leader can stretch further to embrace the extremes while still being able to return to the origin, the centre, the balance to re-establish the norms of the team. This is an infinite task in that it never ends.

Do we need another management model?

There have been hundreds of leadership models. They all analyse individual aspects of the leadership task. This is exactly the problem – they analyse. They don't look at the overall picture. Consequently, there are a lot of management models and most were devised in the 20th century – the most scientific and yet most unbalanced period of humanity. Let's just look at some of the management models, so we can understand where they fall short. There are the 'Three Freds'.

Frederick Winslow Taylor – scientific management theory

Taylor was a mechanical engineer who believed that human beings could work much more efficiently. He is widely accepted as the inventor of time and motion studies and latterly of ergonomics. His theories of workplace productivity became the recruiting sergeant for trade unionism.

Taylor's scientific management model consisted of four principles:

1 Replace custom and practice work methods with those based on a scientific study of the tasks.
2 Select, train and develop each employee scientifically, rather than leaving them to be trained passively by the culture. This is a way that custom and practice are promulgated.
3 Provide detailed scrutiny and oversight of each employee to ensure this remains the case. This is the birthplace of micromanagement.
4 Divide and bureaucratize work so managers and workers are discrete units. Managers apply scientific management principles to planning the work and the workers perform the tasks.

In this model, all workers are reduced to individual units, whose economic value can be measured. Unsurprisingly, this model began to break down as workers resented the all-pervasive measurement. This resulted in mistrust of management who were forever attempting to re-time a job based on the very best workers. This approach was satirized in culture by Fritz Lang's *Metropolis*, Chaplin's *Modern Times* and the Boulting Brothers' *I'm All Right Jack*.

Frederick Herzberg – hygiene and motivating factors

A more enlightened thinker for the 20th century was Frederick Herzberg, a psychologist who had an enormous influence on business management. He was the originator of the hygiene/motivation model of management. He was also the first to have a pivot theory at the centre of his model. Herzberg split environmental factors into hygiene and motivating factors.

Hygiene factors do not motivate, but their absence can demotivate. These factors can be anything from clean toilets and comfortable chairs, to a reasonable level of pay and job security. He said they were 'company policy and administration, supervision, interpersonal relationships, working conditions, salary, status, and security'.[3] This explained why workers were not necessarily satisfied with good conditions. They just accepted them as normal. This then becomes a sort of zero around which motivation pivots.

Motivational factors could involve job recognition, potential for promotion or even the work in itself. Herzberg describes them as 'orientations toward money, recognition, competition, and the dictates of other people, and the latter includes challenge, enjoyment, personal enrichment, interest, and self-determination'.[4] The presence of these can motivate for sure, but unclean toilets can only demotivate.

He termed the hygiene factors 'extrinsic' – something external you expect to receive. The motivators are something 'external' you expect to receive because it is inherently interesting or enjoyable, an internal reward.

Fred Fiedler – contingency management theory

Then, there's the Viennese Fred, Fred Fiedler, one of the leading researchers in industrial and organizational psychology. He came up with contingency management theory. Fiedler based his theories on the idea that effective leadership was directly related to the traits displayed by the leader themselves.

The great thing about Fiedler is that he says there's no one approach that suits every situation and every organization. Instead, three general variables determine leadership and structure: the size, the various levels and the technology of the organization.

In this model, leaders need to adapt their style for any given situation. This requires situational fluency to focus on the alignment of the team and achieving a good fit in all projects and situations. Ultimately, under this theory, there is no one best way to do things. But it is not the size of the organization that matters, it's how balanced the leadership is.

Apart from 'the Freds', there are other theories listed below.

The learning organization

The emphasis in this theory is on collaboration. This covers teamwork, information sharing and empowerment. The essential underlying component of this idea is that change is accelerating. So, the key variable for all organizational success is the rate at which change can be digested. This is determined by how fast the organization can learn.

Bringing us up to more contemporary thinkers, we have Peter Senge. *Harvard Business Review* called his book *The Fifth Discipline*[5] one of the seminal management books of the previous 75 years and he was named 'Strategist of the Century' by *Journal of Business Strategy*.

And they were right to award him the accolades. His idea was that too many businesses are engaged in an endless search for a heroic leader who can deliver change.

Senge's theory is that most efforts to change are hampered by resistance created by the cultural habits of the previous system. There are four challenges in initiating change:

1 There must be a compelling case for change.
2 There must be time to change.
3 There must be help during the change process.
4 As the barriers to change fall, new problems shouldn't replace them.

Senge says learning organizations are continually learning to see the big picture. Only those able to adapt quickly will be able to excel. Learning organizations have two conditions. The first is the ability to design the organization to match the outcomes. Second is the ability to correct any mismanagement to change to the desired outcome.

Thing One and Thing Two

Douglas McGregor, in his book *The Human Side of Enterprise*,[6] identified an environment where employees are motivated via authoritative direction and control or integration and self-control, which he called Theory X (also called *kick 'em hard*) and Theory Y (also called *dangle the carrot*).

The Australians made a contribution to this in the form of Elton Mayo, a clinical psychologist who worked with shell-shocked soldiers from the First World War. Mayo improved productivity by changing environmental conditions, which include things like lighting, temperature and break time. He then changed variables that he thought would have a negative effect on satisfaction, like the length of the workday. What he noticed appeared contradictory. Regardless of the change, good or bad, worker satisfaction always increased.

Mayo's conclusion was illuminating. Performance from the team improved when workers received more attention – good or bad. This was the basis for his human relations theory, which suggested that employees were motivated by social factors, like personal attention or being part of a group.

Influence of environment

One factor linking all these management/leadership models is their longitudinal element. Fred Taylor's model assumed an almost total control of the working environment. Control means measurement. Fred Herzberg's model of controlling hygiene and motivators still assumes a high degree of leadership control. As we move to Fred Fiedler though, there's a growing recognition that leadership doesn't just face the demands of leading the team. The leadership environment is increasingly hard to control because the flexibility demanded by customer sensitivity is so much greater. The growth of zero-hours contracts and flexible working also undermines the notion of total leadership control. The contingency management model and the learning organization are more modern techniques that allow environment change to be accommodated.

This is like the difference between a powerboat and a sailboat. The former needs some consideration of the environment. The latter though needs total consideration. The skippering of a yacht requires this essential awareness of balance. Is there too much weight at the back of the boat? Is the boat in balance laterally? Are the sails trimmed to optimum? An inexperienced crew will not feel comfortable heeled right over, even if the boat is efficient.

The sailboat model also applies in a modern social media environment. Modern leaders need to be aware of the conversations around the company's brand, competitors, shareholders and stakeholders even if they don't respond with direct intervention – for example, share discussion sites like *Motley Fool* and employee sites like *Glassdoor*. Teams are not just affected by facts. Perceptions matter, too.

Now more than ever before, leaders need to be situationally fluent to detect and sense a lack of balance. This level of sensitivity may sound a bit precious, and leaders don't always need to act, but inaction should be a considered rather than a default choice.

What they all have in common

All these leadership and management models feature one thing in common – they are reductive or analytical. They fail to recognize that efficient leadership must be about balance. Of course, we're not saying that leaders need to be in a state of balance at all times. That would be quite impossible anyway. What we are saying is that the leader has a critical role to play in being able to balance the team by recognizing the importance of the centre. Being located at the balance point is the fastest way to get to all extremes. If the leader senses imbalance, the quickest way to correct it is by moving the emphasis to the opposite end of the scale.

Being located at the balance point is the fastest way to get to all extremes.

The benefits of balance

To develop any capacity requires repetition and practice. This tends to be the focus when trying to improve performance. Seldom does anyone look at the opposite of this. What is the opposite of an activity? It's rest. High-performance athletes spend a great deal of time resting. The same is true of creativity. If you want extreme insight, then you also need the opposite. You have to allow the mind to stop and repair itself. This is not always a logical choice. If you want to be better, the usual instinct is to try harder. But speak to any golf pro. There is a magical moment, when golfers are asked to experiment by trying to hit the ball 3/10 rather than 12/10 hard. The result is often miraculous, with the ball travelling further and more accurately. Why? Because golf is not a game of strength, and nor is leadership. There's a clue in the last sentence. It's supposed to be a game. It's supposed to be fun. Why? Because every experimental study shows that people perform better when they're enjoying what they do. They're more relaxed. They're more confident. They bear stress more easily. They use less effort. This is why it's game-changing.

Game-changing performances cannot be achieved without reframing and a change of attitude. Why? Because if performance increase is a conscious effort, it is unsustainable. It needs to be a habit. Habits are unconscious and, by their very nature, sustainable, because the individuals are unaware of making a conscious effort.

It is the very presence of the left brain or scientific mind that invalidates and undermines the right brain or conceptual mind. This is the very source of the imbalance that then manifests as behaviour. If we are steeped only in a scientific, reductionist model of leadership, then we are de facto unbalanced. To achieve balance, we have to accept that we don't need either reductionism or conceptualism – we need both in balance and the equilibrium we seek must become a habit for it to be sustainable.

Habits and instincts

If we're going to change behaviour, we need to understand why it is so embedded and difficult to achieve. This is where habits come in. It's been said that excellence is a habit and that habits are what you do most frequently. To move easily into a different approach requires the ability to change habits and to understand willpower. The *Oxford English Dictionary* defines a habit as 'a settled or regular tendency or practice, especially one that is hard to give up'. So, any practice or activity can be a habit if it is often repeated, but to the point of total assimilation. It defines instinct as 'an innate, typically fixed pattern of behaviour in animals in response to certain stimuli'. An instinct tends to be acquired innately without any formal training, instruction or experience. They sound very similar and they are.

They can be both good and bad. Good, in that they enable a person or team to maintain their position with relative ease. Bad, in that if you need performance improvement, you have to unlock the system, change it and re-lock it.

Whether someone is behaving instinctively or out of habit is immaterial. Both can be reprogrammed and changed. But what is it that makes change happen?

Timing and psychology

Let's look at gym membership.[7] The gym, fitness and health club market is valued at around $27 billion[8] in the US. The total number of gym members in the US alone stands at just over 50 million. Globally, they account for $75.7 billion in revenue annually.

The vast majority of people taking out gym membership do so in January. The majority of these will not last five months. In fact, 4 per cent of new gym members don't even make it past the end of January. Then another 14 per cent drop out by the end of February. So, February is a better time to join than January. Women are more likely to drop out than men. Among those who joined a gym and dropped out within the first year, women accounted for 14 per cent versus just 8 per cent for men. Gym owners expect only about 18 per cent of people who buy memberships to use them consistently. In fact, to be profitable, they need about 10 times as many members as they have capacity for.

There's a strong angle to building habits around other people. 44 per cent of gym-goers exercise with one other person. The gym is also a place to meet new people. 30 per cent of members admit that they never actually break a sweat. They're too busy chatting up others.

Willpower

There's no doubt that some can achieve change through sheer willpower. But not everyone has this level of drive. Chances are, if the task is not enjoyable, then it will not be sustainable. You can see this played out every year in gym memberships. People, when rested, are full of resolve, but then lack willpower once they are back under habitual strain.

The American Psychological Association[9] believes that almost a third of Americans think willpower is the most significant barrier to change.

Lack of willpower isn't the only reason you might fail to reach your goals. It's the inability to defer gratification. Or to put it another way, resist short-term temptations to meet long-term goals.

Marshmallows

One of the most famous tests used to predict the outcome of children's education is Walter Mischel's Marshmallow Test.[10] This is where children are told that if they don't eat a marshmallow that's placed in front of them, they will be given another if they can wait. This is held to be a reliable indicator of whether kids can exert self-discipline to forgo rewards in favour of a bigger reward later. The control of these 'hot emotions' with the Marshmallow Test is now legendary.

The correlation is clear, but what we really need now is an adult marshmallow test for those who would lead boards and governments. These boardroom marshmallows would look like unethical behaviour that boosts short-term profits. The cabinet marshmallows are the short-term popularity that comes with fiscal laxity. We need bigger and different marshmallows.

June Tangney at George Mason University in the US compared willpower by asking undergraduate students to complete questionnaires.[11] The research found the students' grade-point averages correlated directly to the self-control scores. So, the better your relationship skills with yourself, the better they are with others.

Researchers at Duke University found those with high self-control in childhood carried it into adulthood.[12] They had greater financial security, physical and mental health, fewer substance-abuse problems and fewer criminal convictions.

Can you strengthen willpower?

In short, yes. It's a lot easier to control willpower on any one specific task if you're not having to use it for something else. So, those with multiple challenges are likely to be less able to focus willpower on any one thing. This means not having to use your willpower all the time. So, anything that's likely to cause a temptation to break willpower must be avoided. For instance, those trying to achieve discipline in an office must hide or avoid anything that reminds them of ill-discipline. This is sometimes why getting rid of backmarkers can raise overall performance. It takes away the temptation of underachievers to underachieve by removing the most underachieving.

Not many people can use their willpower all the time. It needs to be rested like any other part of the body.

Not many people can use their willpower all the time. It needs to be rested like any other part of the body. If an athlete is constantly trying to beat a new time, then progress is unlikely. This is because a lack of recovery time can increase the chances of injury.

Imagination is also a powerful tool for improving willpower. The body responds as much to imagined situations as it does to real ones. Those imagining food are far more likely to be hungry. Those imagining exercise will be healthier. Those imagining being relaxed will be more relaxed.

It's not just a case of imagining something related to what you feel. Imagining anything other than what you're trying to avoid is useful. So bizarrely, those who can convert a lack of willpower into daydreaming can also make progress.

Roy Baumeister points out that dieting is a way of maintaining a depleted state.[13] As a result, something unusual happens. The dieter feels everything more intensely because by now the tolerance has been reduced *for everything*. This then reinforces the person's perception that they're unable to maintain willpower. Effectively, this is using your imagination against you.

In *Winter Notes on Summer Impressions*,[14] Dostoevsky said:

> Try to pose for yourself this task: not to think of a polar bear, and you will see that the cursed thing will come to mind every minute.

This means you need to control unwanted thought as it threatens to intrude. That gives you control. In Mischel's marshmallow study, many of the 'high delayers' resisted eating the marshmallow by distracting themselves. They did this by covering their eyes with their hands, or turning around in their chairs so they couldn't see the enticing object, or singing to themselves.

Therefore, busy people find it easier to maintain willpower because they are not constantly trying to use it. They are distracted by other things.

Enemies to building willpower

Stress is simply a clear and present imbalance in state. It badly depletes willpower because people tend to fall back on ingrained habits to help them. Stress is essentially having the normal cardinal points temporarily removed. So, individuals replicate them with old habits in order to cope.

It also creates physical effects, increasing the amount of the hunger hormone Ghrelin.[15] This hormone is particularly implicated in the disruption of circadian rhythm, or lack of sleep.[16] This inhibits glucose-stimulated insulin secretion from the pancreas. This makes you hungry and promotes fat storage. In short, relaxed people find it easier to burn more fat.

But what is stress? One thing we can say about its characteristics is that it's not routine. If it was, it would be normal, ie not stress-inducing. So, we can say stress is a non-habitual set of events that is temporarily disorientating. Coping means re-injecting routine. This is why early-stage dieters (or substance abusers trying to get 'clean') often relapse into old habits. New habits have not yet been imprinted and so the stress induces a return to previous behaviour.

Let's take an example of stress. Supposing you have an important exam or business presentation tomorrow. Your grade or your chance of promotion depends entirely on your performance. Your body responds by boosting stress hormones like cortisol. This boosts cravings for carbohydrates because they lower cortisol levels. This is why you crave chocolate or ice cream, which makes you fat, and gives you diabetes and heart disease. Alcohol is also a depressant that lowers cortisol. Getting the picture?

The enormity of the task

Another reason for failure to impose willpower is that often people feel overwhelmed by the enormity of the task. A way of dealing with this is to break the goal down into manageable pieces. This is in a similar way to basic physical training say, for instance with running.

Trying to please others

It takes effort to suppress your personality, preferences and behaviours. Not surprisingly, doing so depletes willpower. Mark Muraven[17] of Albany University in New York found that people who exert this kind of self-control to please others were more easily depleted. When it comes to willpower, these people-pleasers may find themselves at a disadvantage compared with others.

Why this is not taught in schools and universities – some of the most stressful places – is difficult to explain. Maybe it's because there's no easy or right answer. Each person needs to prepare themselves in their own way. Or maybe it's because high achievers do not experience the same problems, therefore do not prioritize it.

Inability to perform in the previous way

This is typically the sort of change forced by ageing. When someone can no longer perform physically in the same way, they are forced to change roles. For this reason, improvements seldom occur during times of economic advancement or market dominance. There's simply no need to change.

Summary

There have been many responses to the challenge of how to make leadership more balanced and effective. This was especially true of the 20th century and its drive for greater efficiency. Unfortunately, they have all focused on the method as being a scientific, Western reductionist model to analyse the problem and come up with a response to a specific issue, rather than addressing the challenge as a whole. This intellectualization has eclipsed a more holistic approach.

The emphasis of study has been on making leadership more efficient in the context of tangible outcomes. This is to say that the only role of the leader is the stewardship of productivity. This is, of course, one of the roles, but it is also there to uphold the values of the group.

Even when leadership does become more efficient, no attempt is made at how to ensure this becomes sustainable. This is where habit and willpower come in. These remain dominant indicators of leadership success, but so little is included about these areas in formal education.

Stress creates an imbalance in the holistic system and it's a factor in addressing leadership outcomes, eg for pilots or cabin crew suffering jet lag who have higher levels of stress because of the environmental factors.

Many of the management or leadership models have focused on individuals as machines to be scientifically managed or deconstructed. These have their uses in understanding human psychology, for example in the area of willpower. They do not, however, focus on the bigger picture to recognize that leaders are subjected to multiple vectors. All of these are constantly destabilizing and the pursuit of overall balance might be a valid goal. The fulcrum point is zero and it is the beginning and end of an infinite human goal.

We can't achieve leadership change, though, without understanding that much of leadership is a habit and to change that requires willpower. We need to understand the psychology of willpower and how to bring about change.

The complexity of this task is challenging and has attracted the attentions of some of the greatest figures in human history. This is what we explore in the next chapter.

CHAPTER FOUR

Introducing 'zero' models

How can we simplify the problems of leadership? Where has this been done before in our history and our culture? How do we divide up multiple areas to make sense of complex, intersecting issues? How do we use these to identify imbalance?

So, we've seen that imbalance has been a problem for centuries and latterly we've sought to achieve greater efficiency via the application of more and more scientific thinking.

But like all thinking, it has been done before and often better. Two inspiring examples of 'balanced greatness' can be seen in Descartes and da Vinci. Both these 16th-century thinkers helped ignite the Renaissance with the way they joined up duality.

One of da Vinci's most famous works was the Vitruvian Man (Figure 4.1). The drawing, in pen and ink on paper, depicts a male figure in two superimposed positions with his arms and legs apart and simultaneously inscribed in a circle and square.

FIGURE 4.1 The Vitruvian Man

The image is interesting on multiple levels. First, it provides the perfect example of da Vinci's interest in proportion. The navel is the centre of the circle whose arcs perfectly encompass the outstretched feet and hands. Second, it expresses the duality of art and science represented in man and the juxtaposition of the circle and square.

There have been many attempts over the years to understand the composition of da Vinci's principles. It is this that inspired our thinking 400 years later. What was he really saying? He was juxtaposing two essentially opposed concepts. In Vitruvian Man, art and science. Organic and inorganic. Awe-inspiring infinite and the mundane. Even the symmetry of man himself represents a type of divine balance. The superimposed imagery suggests a juxtaposition of the static with the dynamic. Even the layout of the drawing suggests the symbolism of the cross or the mystery of the X.

Introducing the infinite model

Supposing we zoom out from the Vitruvian Man to create an elemental version. We would have an 'X' surrounded by a circle with two intersecting lines. We'd have a circle of zero at the centre. This would express a neutral or balanced position between two polar opposites (Figure 4.2).

The model permits some degree of subjective calibration. This might be assumptive but it allows relative positioning against the polarities. It also allows the creation of 'vectors' or directions of travel from quadrant to quadrant. This is important as full and opposite action can inform the return to balance. This is particularly important when diagnosing the imbalance and the vector required to address it. Part of the leader's responsibility in maintaining balance is the ability to preserve capacity to be ready in the event of the unforeseen occurring. This is analogous to a Premier League manager who trains the team hard to build stamina so they can play to 70 per cent of their capacity. The further within comfortable limits, the fewer mistakes. The best-performing teams are where leadership philosophy is embedded in the culture. This means every individual needs to recognize the importance of taking responsibility.

FIGURE 4.2 The infinite model

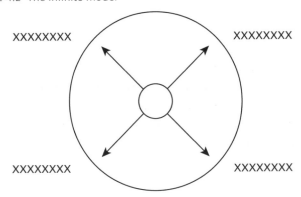

FIGURE 4.3 The hearts and minds model

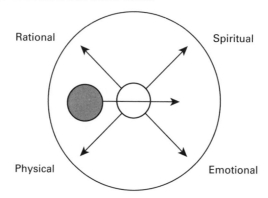

The model is also useful because it doesn't just focus on the individual. It can be used to assess individuals and teams together or separately. It can be used at the company, organization, national or international level.

The best-performing teams are where leadership philosophy is embedded in the culture.

Let's overlay some opposing continua on the model. Supposing we introduce the rational and the emotional, intersecting with the physical and the spiritual. This could give us what we might call the hearts and minds model (Figure 4.3).

The emphasis is on balance

Let's say we start with the proposition that our imbalance is created by an overemphasis on the rational and the physical. This might be a fair assumption about the imbalance that we saw in the run-up to the financial crash. This is represented by the circle of the model. If we wanted to correct that balance, it would involve applying doses of the spiritual and emotional to bring it back to centred. Could this be the reason why so many knowledge workers will unwind by going to the theatre, pub, recital, etc after intensive work?

One cardinal point does not supplant the other entirely, the scales are intentionally infinite. Positive and negative readings are discouraged. One is not good, the other is not bad. The plus or minus scales could be labelled *alpha* and *beta*. They are there to calibrate either side of the neutral or zero state. Humans are not better off if they are purely rational or purely emotional. They are best when they have all four aspects in balance, which is the infinite challenge.

The axes

Let's first explore the meaning of the axes and some of the basic rules. This model is reflexive and also illustrates homeostatic defence.[1] Travelling towards any extremity works against the natural state, so the body will always seek to balance or defend itself. Spiritual thinking is credible only if leavened by rationalism. Rational thinking can often be of help with emotional understanding. Spiritual enlightenment often reveals itself when athletes are reaching their maximum physical capacity. Those who are overly rational are not much fun to work with. Or might even be considered by other people to be 'mad'. See Sherman Klump in *The Nutty Professor*.

The point of logic is to prove that it, too, is as limited as faith.

At the heart of the model is an axis of human challenge. Before we continue, a word of caution. All models are limited in their use because there are limits to rationality. In a way, this is also the point we're making. The point of logic is to prove that it, too, is as limited as faith.

The spiritual

There's a reason that the spiritual is uppermost in the model. This is because it is the cardinal point that is most conspicuous by its absence, most abundant by its presence. More of this duality later. It is also the most difficult to encapsulate. Like trying to capture smoke. What do we mean by spiritual? We can't measure it. We can't order it. We can't teach it. We can't legalize it. It's just not legitimate, but we all know it matters in the right measure. If the leader starts spouting the need for Zen, we might question what spirits they are on!

We know the phrases 'high spirits' and 'team spirit'. We even know the word 'inspiration'. But what does it mean to be spiritual? It refers to our soul, a receptacle of life force, zest or energy, and appetite for life.

We can have a spirit of compromise, a spirit of 1776, a spirit of enterprise, a Dunkirk spirit, a spirit of which is a symbol of intent or mood. You can get into the spirit of something. Your troops can fight with spirit. You can have team spirit. Somebody can be absent but with us in spirit. We can act within the spirit of the law. Our spirits can be lifted and broken and transformed and ignited.

So, let's look at what it's *not*, if we come momentarily to its opposite, the physical. Athletes, especially runners, often refer to themselves as being in 'the zone' – a mental state where they feel themselves to be incorporeal, almost outside of their physical body. In this space they feel calm, comfortable and balanced. The state can be predicted after an initial phase of exercise. Runners might feel this state of elation in the first mile. Cyclists might reach it in the first five miles.

In any case, this illustrates what we're getting at with the spiritual. It's where an activity, place, team or even a piece of art can induce a transcendent state. This is, frankly, all a bit tricky to describe. Not because of a lack of words, but because it's something that is experienced through *feeling*. It's a sense of the supernatural, something that's mythical or mystic. This is what Daniel Pink calls flow.[2]

In flow, people live so deeply in the moment, and feel so utterly in control, that their sense of time, place, and even self, melts away.

Sometimes, it manifests as a sense of belonging. Sometimes as contentment. It can be induced and it is reflexive. As much as people for instance have their best ideas in the shower. The shower can therefore be said to be an inductive location, where good ideas might come about. Places of worship are the same. People don't have to be in a place of worship to feel spiritually connected, but it frequently helps.

The rational

Although this is one of the youngest cardinal points, it's the one we've been infatuated with since the Enlightenment. It's what we've used to make our lives easier and more productive. It keeps us healthy and increasingly living longer lives. It's Mr Spock, from the show *Star Trek*, and his relentlessly logical thinking. It wears a suit and tie. It's respectable. It's valued. It has standing in the local and national community. It's the cardinal point you can take home to introduce to your parents. You'll find it resident in our banks, garages, schools, universities, factories, farms, offices, armed forces and yes, sometimes even our politicians. We're all very comfortable with this because it's literally what we know and can prove. It all adds up. It is smirking and self-satisfied. It is the basis for science as sequential, repeatable and verifiable. It exists. It can be measured. It has a value that can be assessed. It explains things. It gives us all our tables (periodic, logarithmic, sine/cosine, tangent, navigational, celestial and water). We can put this on a balance sheet. We can teach it. It's at its strongest in mathematics and in physics.

The emotional

We know mankind has had feelings since it was first able to express them. From the earliest cave paintings, we can see that man has had a desire to express emotion. From the Enlightenment onwards, the rise of logic made anything emotional appear to be weaker. It became important to suppress emotions and not to give in to them as a matter of self-control. It was seen as part of the process of education. Somewhere in the last 20 years this has changed dramatically. Incidences of anger, for instance, are the highest we've seen for generations.[3] Of all of the axes, this is the most explosive. It can destroy relationships or it can make them. Perhaps the most common emotion of all when expressed about leadership is frustration.

We also know that this is the one area that leaders find real, practical difficulty dealing with. Some leaders will avoid confrontation with their teams. Teams, in turn and for obvious reasons, avoid confrontation with leadership. This is exacerbated by the flow of communication, but not conversation. Employees will be frequently subjected to large amounts of communication, but very seldom will anyone actually talk to them.

The physical

Another ancient cardinal, physical prowess has long been associated with leadership. This is particularly prized in the military. It still matters greatly because height is associated with authority and loudness with confidence. This explains why CEOs for instance are significantly taller than the rest of the population.[4] It also shows the battles that females are up against when gaining access to leadership groups. Google the word 'leader' and look at the images. You will see people standing, striding, wearing suits, in offices or figuratively climbing things. You will not see images of the disabled, the elderly, although you will increasingly see more women and ethnic minorities. You will not, however, see images of imams, rabbis, priests, nurses, doctors, farmers, engineers, miners or firefighters. To look at these images, we would conclude that leadership is a professional or executive profession. It is a male profession. It is mainly for those between the ages of 30 and 60. It is mainly for white men. If you don't look like a leader defined in those terms, then you are often told that you are clearly not a leader. Instead you are called a feminist or a racist, who must favour quotas or other artificial methods of displacing the former group of leaders. This has to change.

The quadrants

Challenges in one quadrant can be countered by full and opposite application of opposing forces. Someone going through a divorce may be said to be spiritually and emotionally challenged, and may benefit from a period of physical and intellectual activity.

In many respects, this book is inspired by the great John C Maxwell's books on leadership. His volume of work is centred on the upper right zone in the spiritual/emotional quadrant. This perhaps is why they are so avidly read by overly rational/physical leaders. Maxwell's background as a religious pastor facilitates the shifting of the approach from bottom left to top right of the model. Of course, this trajectory passes through zero on its way to the opposite quadrant.

Maxwell's work is illuminated by his divinity training, which encourages contemplation of the infinite. There is, though, a gravitational pull back to the lower left quadrant where the lack of holistic thinking drives division. Division drives ego at the top and the bottom. So many leaders are either effortlessly successful or 'out to prove a point'. The education required for zero leadership should teach us how to achieve greater levels of balance.

Our argument is that leadership has become anchored in the bottom left quadrant, where economic rationalism, at any cost, has dominated the notion of 'good' leadership. But this quadrant has no home for long-term qualitative values. Short-term, quantitative goals dominate this space and consistently drive us into catastrophic leadership failures.

Many inspirational leaders are rated in the upper right quadrant. For instance, Eric Schmidt's *The Trillion Dollar Coach* attributes the success of Google to love.[5] His book is about how one man, Bill Campbell, loved the team at Google and many other great companies like Apple, Amazon, Intuit, Kleiner Perkins into a winning formula. Love, he says, 'belongs in the board room and in the business but we don't teach this.'[6] Love belongs in the Oval Office. Love belongs in your life, your community, in your business, your organizations and your ideals. Today we complain about the leaders we have and rail at the absence of good leadership. We are fully justified in doing so. Our leaders are failing us. But, fixing this may not be as simple as ticking a box, whether we are voting for a politician or exercising a shareholder proxy.

But this is not the whole story. Of course, emotional/spiritual pressure, when applied to the rational/physical position, pushes the leadership back to the origin. This is where leadership needs to be. It needs to be capable of navigating all quadrants but must always be able to return to zero.

Not everything that counts can be counted. Not everything that can be counted, counts.

John Hope Bryant's *Love Leadership: The new way to lead in a fear-based world*[7] is a great book. It deals with issues affecting the poor and financial literacy. While this is an interesting read, it is primarily a political and economic analysis, but his thinking is informative here. Because love is the greatest of all things that cannot be counted, calculated, codified, managed, measured, standardized, reported upon, built into compliance, legislated for, mandated or directed.

The rational–spiritual quadrant

This quadrant is full of paradox. It deals with what we might call highly relevant ambiguities. This might be embodied in the phrase: 'The rules are made for the obedience of fools and the guidance of the wise.' It is perhaps one of the most puzzling areas of leadership rules – that they should be applied most of the time until one has to use judgement. Not everything that counts can be counted. Not everything that can be counted, counts.

The rational–physical quadrant

This is the refuge of the left-brained analytical person. It has thrived since the Enlightenment and is often referred to as 'the industrial model'. It is the home of the modern education system, which was created by, and in the interests of, industry. It is fundamentally mechanistic. It sorts all participants by year of manufacture rather than ability or skill set. The method is fundamental to our educational systems today and is ruled by tests, which themselves seek to separate and divide by ever more precise methods of parsing and division into categories of expertise. It drives us all into ever deeper silos.

This is the home of compare, contrast, analyse processes. When we educate people, we seek to boost the logical, the rational and the intellectual. We define thinking as a reductive process. We teach people to break down problems into smaller problems and those problems into smaller ones yet, in order to solve them. The aim is dissection not unification. The goal is to isolate the smallest critical components, not to find ways to connect them together into a big picture. This is a land of spreadsheets that has no place for impressionist landscapes or surrealist paintings.

There is, of course, an equal and opposite process, that of synthetic logic, which seeks to zoom out of the problem to ask the wider questions. This is embodied in the Toyota '5 Whys',[8] developed by the founder of the Japanese car company, which sought to ask five times why there was a problem. This has the effect of raising each observation to a higher or even the strategic level.

The model takes no account of the subconscious brain and does not explain why so many thinkers report epiphanies that come when they are on their own, not in the workplace and, interestingly, *not trying.*[9]

The central proposition of this book is not that the rational is our enemy. It is, as Einstein put it, that the rational mind is a faithful servant, but the intuitive mind is a sacred gift. We honour the servant but have forgotten the gift. We need the rational but we needn't let the rational take oxygen away from all the other quadrants.

The spiritual–emotional quadrant

Traditionally, this is where you'd find inspirational leadership. It's not difficult to understand why leaders with strong emotional and spiritual scores tend to be popular with their teams. It's less clear how popular they are with investors and voters.

Emotionally and spiritually led leaders often find it difficult to make tough people decisions. They also miss key trends in the analysis of data. They are, however, typically good at managing teams. They collaborate well, often at the expense of personal achievement.

Love is that gift that should be available to leadership to be used in conjunction with the other skills, but it isn't. The absence is costing us dearly. It's no longer enough just to be an intelligent analytical leader. Of course, this helps. But the indivisible quality is that of the resilience, good humour and happiness that only true love can bring. Families stay together because of love; organizations can too.

The physical–emotional quadrant

The human being is not a linear machine. It will not run and run without rest. Although this is self-evidently the case, it does not stop individuals from personally and persistently testing the theory. It usually ends in temporary exhaustion. Sometimes, it ends up with chronic cases of ME unless full and opposite treatment is applied. This is the home of a man of a certain age with a ruddy face, who is carrying too much weight and is angry at all the little things. He explodes when he cannot find his keys, which are in his pocket. This is the person who needs to feel the energy in a room but cannot even feel the pain in their gut that signals the onset of a cancer.

One of the great problems with challenges in the physical–emotional quadrant is that quite frequently, the subject has become so cognitively impaired that they have no idea how cognitively impaired they have become. This requires self-management, but the internal datum is notoriously unreliable for the above reason. The way to combat this is either with regular 'hygiene' breaks or with a buddy system that allows the leader to gain feedback from a peer either inside or outside the organization.

How the model explains imbalance

The acceleration of the physical/rational has been seen every-where. In science, in commerce, in industry, in healthcare, in transportation, in energy, etc. It has forced people to keep up or be left behind. Incidentally, many have chosen this latter path and have been much happier. Perhaps for being more spiritually/ emotionally aligned?

Not all change needs to be kept up with. Technology comes and goes often without being used. Landfill sites are full of VCRs that no one learned to program. Breakers' yards full of cars whose dimmable dashboards were never mastered. Recycling centres full of washing machines whose many programmes were never used.

Nevertheless, the emphasis of this quadrant has led to a percep-tion (of those in the quadrant at least) of superiority. This is a land of division, of comparison, of us versus them. Whether it be Trump supporters talking to Democrats or British Brexiteers talking to Remainers or those in China who stand for centralization of power or decentralization of power, there is always a clear feeling that the opposing parties are talking down to each other. 'Anywhere'-living, educated rationalism looks down on 'somewhere'-living, unedu-cated patriotism. They treat each other with equal contempt.

Why has this become so common? Why have we lost the ability to be respectful? There's no doubt that the tone of online debate is harshened by disinhibition – *I'm going to say this because no one can see who I am*. But this doesn't explain the clashes in face-to-face environments. Could it be that we have tired of rationalism and its constant and relentless interruptions, comparisons and complexities? Could it be that we see raw emotion as a holiday from rationalism? This might explain the phenomena of recrea-tional violence and drug-taking, which deliver emotional, physical and spiritual rewards at the expense of rational thought.

Rationalism and efficiency applied to relationships

Relationships in general are in decline, and in young men, massively so.[10] Young men are having relationships, just not with anyone else. This means they are becoming less experienced with them. This is potentially harmful for a number of reasons, not just their leadership potential.

If the theory is correct, that each polarity of the model is homeostatically defended, then could it be that those two extremities are causing each other? That somehow, as the workplace has become so rational, it has displaced spiritual and emotional behaviour to areas beyond the workplace? Could it be that the absence of any love in the workplace degrades the need for it outside of the workplace? Is love now seen as something that interrupts efficiency? People won't date or marry anyone who might not benefit their career. Does the absence of love facilitate the reduction of relationships to transactions?

Although 16 per cent of couples met in the workplace, as many as 40 per cent admit to casual relationships with people they work with.[11] Generally, couples who met as a result of a workplace relationship are in decline, compared with couples who meet online. According to one dating agency, in the latter instance, 40 per cent of the single population use online dating.[12]

In the future, the internet will broker all main relationships

Even as it stands, the internet is being used for meetings – especially when working from home – it can send you food, it can allow teams to collaborate in real time, it can handle business transactions, provide accounting detail, even tell you when to stop working. Domestically, it can store all your personal data, offer you people to date, do your washing, entertain you, clothe you, exercise and accommodate you. What might be the effect on leadership as this dehumanized intermediation accelerates? It could be that leadership must work more remotely as it did during the coronavirus outbreak, managing at a distance and learning different techniques. Invariably, this means a narrowing of overall assessment criteria to the quantitative and data-based. Data will be the critical element of this because an employer will know more about the work patterns, productivity and accuracy of employees than ever before. Humans, though, are not machines. They will make mistakes. They will be slower and less consistent. There is a growing expectation that the offline world should move as fast as the online one. The evidence that this is making people more impatient is already there.[13]

There is also an increasing tendency to share resources among increasingly single households. In every age group, the number of coupled partnerships living under one roof is declining with the exception of the over-60s.[14]

Communication, but no conversation

There is no doubt that the iPhone generation has increased its amount of communication. There has, though, been a steep decline in conversation. This can be witnessed in almost any modern family who often sits in silence as they access their social and online media. A lack of conversation means a lack of ability to negotiate and to resolve emotional difficulties. It also means a rise in online anger. This anger looks increasingly like the inability to empathize with another's point of view added to the emotional frustration of not being able to do so.

Applying the models to different criteria

What if we now take the hearts and minds axes and replace them with other criteria? The model could then become a meta model where any set of opposites might be placed on it with any other. This would then give us the ability to test one position of balance with another. This is what we will look at next.

Summary

The search for balance is nothing new. It's been going on for centuries. It could even be said to be the very substance of man's history on earth – an infinite pursuit. Our society and culture were heavily based on faith. This was an imbalance that was addressed firstly by the Renaissance and later by the Enlightenment.

The Renaissance was a historical period where learning and art accelerated. This led to widespread educational reform. In politics, it contributed to the development of government and diplomacy, and in science to an increased reliance on observation and reasoning. The Renaissance was best known for its artistic developments and the contributions of artists such as Leonardo da Vinci and Michelangelo.

Its successor, the Enlightenment, started where the Renaissance left off to create a European intellectual movement that focused on reason and individualism. Its leading lights were scientists like Descartes, Locke and Newton, and literary figures including Goethe, Voltaire, Rousseau and economist Adam Smith.

These two great movements represented mankind's best attempts to balance, first against faith, with the application of reason and then yet more science in the 20th century. It almost seems that man, in his desire to create balance, has only ended up creating another kind of imbalance.

The approach of da Vinci and his drawing of the Vitruvian Man inspired our balance model, which we can now apply to different situations. We take the essence of its message and reduce it to intersection of two forces that need to be balanced. These forces move around the fulcrum or a zero state, which we explore next.

CHAPTER FIVE

Zero-state thinking

What is a 'zero' state? How do we get there? Why is it impor-
tant? How can you tell when you've arrived at it? How can it be
applied? What are the benefits? Why do so many great leaders
try to maintain balance? Is this the same as being 'Zen'? How
can it be used to build our resilience and potential?

One of the greatest books on leadership is *The Three Meter*
Zone: Common sense leadership for NCOs by J D Pendry.[1]
He describes three types of soldier: the three-metre, ten-metre
and 100-metre soldier. Each requires different leadership. In the
first group, soldiers don't learn from the leader, they learn from
other soldiers. The leader in each area creates a normative field
in which they set the tone of the behaviour and standards. The
field is an example of the culture being held in balance – whatever equilibrium might be considered for the military. These
balanced fields are powerful.

The most extreme example of this was illustrated by a
Yale researcher, Stanley Milgram.[2] He showed that deference to

authority was so powerful that some participants in his behavioural experiments would routinely administer lethal electric
shocks because they'd been given orders to do so. This illustrates
clearly the normative field that each leader creates around them.
The moment the leader embarks upon morally questionable
behaviour, the normative field is changed.

There's a balance that leadership needs to strike between the
operational/tactical and the strategic/emblematic. Let's simplify
this between *doing* and *being*. In Pendry's model, it's clear that
the leadership has to *do*. They have to set an example. They
need to have a 'to do' list. They need to execute on it and they
need to have a clear set of expectations and values. Of course,
this is true at the 100-metre level as well, excepting that the
proportions and ratios will be different. At the strategic end, the
leader must have a set of values that can be projected. A 'to be'
list, if you like.

Let's see how the zero model could be used in conjunction
with Pendry (Figure 5.1).

This illustrates that the tactical leader would be at your side
'doing' things operating in close support (Figure 5.2).

The strategic leader, however, might be positioned more in the
right-hand quadrant, for example a general who sees the bigger

FIGURE 5.1 The Pendry model A

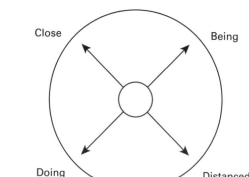

FIGURE 5.2 The manager vs leader model

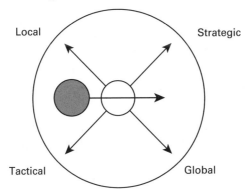

picture. You wouldn't expect the general to be doing the same things as a sergeant. Therefore, imbalance could change by level. We could also express this difference by using it to explain the difference between managers and leaders (Figure 5.3).

Leaders should be capable of operating at both the tactical and the strategic level, managers only at the lower level. This is typically a model where management does a good job of meeting local and tactical needs but fails to understand complete strategic goals. Again, the opposite approach is self-explanatory.

FIGURE 5.3 The Pendry model B

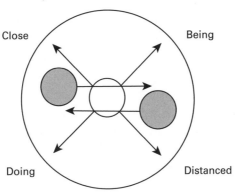

A zero-sum game?

In any group without a designated leader, it is quite possible that there is no visible or obvious leader. American Indian and Aboriginal tribes often remarked that they had no leader until confrontation with colonialists forced them to designate someone to that task.

In modern-day societies, someone in particular usually emerges as a representative. The most common manifest of this is in the context of an American jury. Twelve people are required to elect a representative. Of course, when someone volunteers to lead, this means that some people can then sit back. They can place (or offload) their trust (or responsibility) in someone else. In this respect the leader absolves the team of their personal responsibilities. In theory, this could allow them to specialize, but it can also create another normative field – that of the team rather than the leader. For this reason, non-commissioned officer leadership is given a great deal of thought in the military. It is essential that the normative field is created by formal rather than informal authority. If the latter exceeds the former through any breakdown in trust, then we end up with mutiny. For this reason, the military offers individuals every chance to experience leadership during training, so they can feel the responsibility of leadership. It is hoped that by so doing, they will have greater sympathy with and understanding of the role of leadership.

This illustrates clearly the role of training and role play not only in leadership but in team development, too. It's not enough to train the leader to lead. The team needs to be trained to follow. Without this, a leader may be taken for granted and no matter how stoic they are, the more cynicism they can attract. The cynics and stoics are philosophical schools passed down to us by antiquity, but one can see them at work today. The former are those for whom leadership is grudgingly accepted as a necessary evil. They do not support it, but they do not attack it either. You don't need to look far for this. A new age of cynicism has grown up distrusting the motives of others and showing contempt for accepted standards of honesty or morality. This is an approach where only selfishness motivates human actions, and there is a belief that the world's actions are mainly negative. It's dangerous stuff.

Modern leaders tend to inhabit the stoical group. They are leaders for whom the needs of the team come before their own requirements. Leaders can thus advertise their own capabilities paradoxically by extolling the virtues of their team members. This unselfishness is one of the traits of great leadership. It also explains how great teams can be created. Individual identities are welded together into something bigger. How is this done? Let's look at the ways.

Humour, the ultimate clearance to zero

One of the great shortcomings of all psychometric testing is its inability to recognize key human leadership skills like humour.

All great leaders use humour for communication. When Ronald Reagan's desk was emptied from the Oval Office, it contained written jokes – hundreds of them. When leaders use humour, they display judgement, timing, sensitivity, shared perspective and intelligence. Humour is therefore something we should take seriously in leadership.

The psychology of training is such that people tend to get good at things they like doing. Because work is a social process, it's therefore probable that if you like your team, you'll want to work well with them. Competence follows preference. This can create another circle – a virtuous one where people like their team, therefore they work well together, therefore their skills improve, therefore they become more valuable, therefore they receive higher rewards and therefore they like their work more. Unfortunately, the cycle doesn't work in reverse. When teams are enjoying themselves, they tend to be less focused on the rational/physical realm. This makes them less likely to compare, contrast, analyse and notice difference. Work no longer seems like work and the team enters into 'flow'.[3]

Momentum as a path to zero

Another path to a balanced team may be through the creation of momentum, whether on training tasks or work in progress. Nothing enhances team cohesion quite like pressure of work. This is why so many military organizations keep new recruits busy for their first months in the service. Apart from the fitness benefits, it also allows the meta skills of teamwork to be put in place.

One of the problems with leadership is that it assumes it must come solely from leaders. You are the leader. We are all the leader.

This momentum could be likened to the effect that forward motion has on the stability of a bicycle. A vital element of zero-state thinking is the creation and maintenance of momentum. This creates a gyroscopic effect pushing forces to the centre of the axis. People are still debating what keeps a bicycle vertical.[4] All that matters from our point of view is that it does.

Is the leader responsible?

One of the problems with leadership is that it assumes it must come solely from leaders. You are the leader. We are all the leader. Leadership can never afford to be personally certain. In a quantum superpositioned environment, the provenance of certainty must be mediocrity. Zero leadership doesn't just predict one outcome, it prepares for ALL outcomes. It must be disinterested. Zero preparation speaks to the pre-existing mindset required for key leadership insights.

When someone goes actively in search of creativity, they may find some of it. But most leaders relate that real epiphanies often occur outside the office space, outside the work group and often when not trying. This emphasizes the importance of the zero state as a precondition for creative epiphany.

This is similar to the state of love. The person who searches for love is less likely to be found by it. We don't need leaders with brains or with hearts, we need them with both.

Zero is not 'Zen'

We're not advocating leaders who are totally Zen. Of course, there's a time for that but there's also a time for dynamic, dedicated, focused, passionate, here-and-now leadership. The point here is that no matter how flexible the leader is, they still need to be able to snap back to the zero state. This is not to say that they should choose this at every point. What we're talking about here is balance between the extreme positions, for instance: on a continuum between they, we and I:

'They'   **'We'**   **'I'**
Powerless ◄————————Zero Leader————————► All-powerful

This is the question we addressed about ego. It has to be 'we' not 'me'.

The leader needs to be fluid, agile, active and looking-across, rather than solely drill-down. They should be neutral to events, disinterested and of no fixed opinion. This then allows them latitude for any position. Buddhists call this a state of 'non-attachment'. It means that you are free to deal with all possibilities without being attached to any particular outcome. This attitude then leaves a leader free to harness the power of the decision-making capabilities of the team. Working on the basis that the minority view is where you find the newest and most powerful ideas, leaders must be able to create an environment where minorities can be heard. A leader's job is not only to represent the winners or the majority. The job is to knit together the community so that all can benefit, not just those who have greater numbers.

The leader as 'peace weaver'

All groups of people have factions. This can be down to location in an office, department, skill set or preference. The leader's job is to improve the fate of all by enmeshing everyone in a larger fabric of identity and values. The leader must ensure that these groups come to realize what they have in common. This can be achieved by periodically swapping personnel. The term 'peace weaver' comes from the Anglo-Saxon where women were married into opposing tribes in order to promote peace between them. The more integration, the more likelihood that subcultures will understand each other. The warp and weft of this peace weaving was sometimes intricate to enable strong bonds to be created.

Subcultures can exist within departments, they can also occur within different locations, even on separate floors within the same building. Cultural differences are usually the reason why instructions are either not implemented or carried out in such a way as to be inconsistent with the whole.

What threads in your organization are not woven together, or are fraying or torn? What can you do to repair that communal fabric? This is an Infinite Leader's task.

It is interesting that a powerful archetype from the world of legends has been a 'shield maiden' who is also a peace weaver. Think of Athena who is a goddess of both war and art. She is a symbol of wisdom, freedom and democracy and yet a warrior too. Kathleen Herbert, in her book *Peace-Weavers and Shield Maidens: Women in early English society*,[5] points out that the word *wif* preceded the word wife. The word *wif* stems from the words *wefan*, which means to weave, and *wefta*, which means threads. The ancient Greeks also described the three fates as goddesses who would spin the threads of fate just as a weaver would spin the thread and weave fabric. Those three fates were called Clotho, the spinner, Lachesis, the allotter, and Atropos, the inflexible. This idea captured the notion that the social fabric must be woven together from warp and weft. The toughness of one being balanced by the flexibility of the other. The interests of the majority and the minorities alike must be woven together in order to create something that was both beautiful and durable. Unity can be torn and frayed at times. It may take both the spindle and the spear, the enduring symbols of peace-weaving, to compel opposing elements to come together.

This may sound weird. That would be because it derives from the Old English word *wyrd*, which meant destiny. These words had a deeper meaning in the older root *wert*, which meant to turn or rotate, and *weorp*, which meant the origin of price, value and affinity with identity, honour and esteem. *Wyrdness*, like weirdness, is associated with magic and the ability to conjure forth solutions or premonitions that seem almost impossible or unimaginable.

But what if you applied this thinking to the potential in people? Can you imagine the circumstances under which you might become successful? If so, then you can imagine the circumstances where other people might become successful, that they perhaps become successful in an alternative reality.

Leaders, in this sense, need to be a little *wyrd*, or weird, in order to pick up the threads of truth from all sides to forge a fabric that can include everyone's interest and allegiance.

Who sees change first?

Janet Daly writing in *The Telegraph*[6] points out that leaders seem to believe that because things are not changing for them, they're not changing for everyone else.

Nobody – not even the people who have responsibility for these matters – seems to be aware of how rapidly things are changing and how important adaptation and fluidity are going to be in this metamorphosis.

Perhaps the greatest asset of the neutral state is permeability – or the openness to the situation and what it requires. This is the key thing about leadership vision. It doesn't need to be the leader who has the ideas or even who sees them. The leader just needs to create a culture where ideas can come to life. This means the ability to tolerate diversity, even unconventional thinking. This involves the consideration of unorthodox sources of information and unusual ways of combining the information. Leaders are responsible not just for the environment that allows innovation but also for implementing it. It's the latter part of this that needs the leader's experience. The Australian psychologist Fred Emery put it well when he said, 'Instead of constantly adapting to change, why not change to be adaptive?'[7] That's the leader's key role. They help their teams become adaptive instead of just adaptable.

How can the models help us with this openness?

The openness model

When we're assessing the permeability of leadership to ideas, we know new ideas always arrive via minority views. This is true even when the idea is unanimously adopted. It starts with a minority view then spreads. But the point here is that permeability to diverse thinking and minorities results in more receptivity to innovations. We'll talk more about the philosophy behind this.

The model illustrates that leaders who talk to the same people all the time, especially people like them, are unlikely to spot new ideas. They might copy them, but they're unlikely to discover them (Figure 5.4).

FIGURE 5.4 The openness model

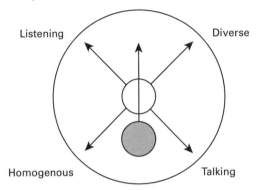

In a similar way, we can use the model to identify egocentric behaviour, by intersecting two different axes – those of me and we, with listening and talking (Figure 5.5). The same procedure can be applied to sustainability.

It also explains why innovation suffers when the leader is egocentric. The needs of the leader take priority over the needs of the team.

FIGURE 5.5 The egocentric model

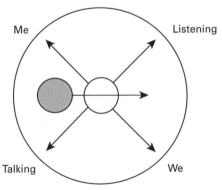

Why does it matter that leaders create a culture that welcomes change?

Because the only real advantage that any team has is its ability to adapt to change. That's why this attitude matters. A time of great change can be like wind blowing on a choppy sea, but this environment, if harnessed correctly, can propel the team greatly. And this is the point, the zero-state leader with few resources is able to harness environmental forces and the talent and potential of the team.

The zero-state potential can have tremendous benefit for team members who are able to take opportunity. When the team is forced into new circumstances and experiences, it can develop new competencies and confidence. This joint development can result in a team becoming unusually bonded while still having an open culture.

When organizations and teams navigate change successfully and openly they create an approach that keeps on winning. Mutual trust grows and it becomes easier to cope with change.

It's tempting to think of change in the abstract, but really what we're talking about is not change, but events. We build teams to cope with events and no two events are the same. Each involves a different set of skills and experiences. The more events, the greater the competencies of the team. This is the reason why zero-state thinking is so important – it can help accelerate not only the team's skills but also the rate at which the team can assimilate change.

Why are some organizations slow to adapt to new ideas? Sometimes, it's down to rigidity and routine of the processes. Take the military for instance. This is based on strict procedures and routines. There is powerful incumbency within the teams. They are designed to have a high level of cohesion with little tolerance of individuality.

The hourglass model of leadership

The Royal Navy has an interesting philosophy in this respect. The hourglass represents the two disciplines that naval leadership represents. In the first half, people are required to follow orders to the letter. This is the discipline required of combat situations where imperatives are paramount. Everyone understands this, but at the higher levels of the leadership something different happens. Leaders have to be allowed to use their initiative and act independently. This is almost the polar opposite of what they learned at the start of their careers.

How can these two seemingly opposite ideas be reconciled? This is the challenge of leadership, to exist at the interface of seemingly irreconcilable ideas. How do leaders do this? Trust and integrity are important to inspire confidence and this works up and down the structure. This can be established only through a consistent application of the values of the team.

The Royal Navy talks about the Nelson Touch. Nelson was its foremost admiral. His approach, of course, relied on discipline, but also on independent thinking and autonomous action. At the Battle of Trafalgar in 1805, there was a plan that Nelson knew would break down once the fight began. His orders then anticipated this – he gave his men one simple maxim: seek out the nearest enemy and engage them closely.

There is a school of thought that the leader should always be part of the team – sit with them, experience what they experience.

Is this a hypocritical approach? Well, yes it is. Leaders have to operate with a greater level of trust. This is why it's such a special position. They must be dedicated to the welfare and well-being of the team.

The hourglass is a symbol of different kinds of leadership skill. The crossover from one side to the next is a vanishing point. It is the zero space we've discussed. It is a portal that operates as a pivot or interface where the leadership paradox becomes visible. It is the point at which the maiden becomes a mother. It is where the boy becomes a man. Oliver Wendell Holmes captured it well when he wrote, 'The young man knows the rules, but the old man knows the exceptions.'[8] It is the point at which yin meets yang, life meets death and heaven meets earth. It is a reminder that radical change is sometimes required. Otherwise all the sand naturally just drops to the bottom container and stays in stasis there. But, somehow, we tend to turn hourglasses over. We change our ways of thinking and begin anew.

Changing cultures

Changing our thinking is hard. The worst thing you can do to an individual, or to a group, is to destroy their belief systems. All cultures, traditions, rituals, honours, rest on a belief system. They exist at the heart of every person and every community. The leader's own 'force field' is an important part of this. The leader needs to be seen to be representing the values of the belief systems their community holds true. This commitment to values and belief systems cannot be expressed by a 'to-do' list. A leader can only express it by a 'to-be' list. You can't show these values. You have to live them. The slightest discrepancy will inevitably invite a loss of confidence in the leader.

This commitment to values and belief systems cannot be expressed by a 'to-do' list. A leader can only express it by a 'to-be' list.

This brings us to a fundamental contradiction in a democracy. You are elected by a majority but then spend your time catering for a minority. In this sense, then, the majority votes for someone who will deal with the minority. It may seem ironic but leaders are elected by their own party as being the best to represent another party.

Why does the minority view matter? Why can't the minority simply be ignored? The simple answer is that the future always arrives through a minority view.

The leader as 'deviant'

All minorities are deviant in so far as they do not represent the norm. The leader's job here is to grant permission for the 'deviancy'. This may sound odd. Frank Zappa got it right when he said, 'Without deviation from the norm, progress is not possible.'[9] If we all have the same views and ideas, there isn't much space for innovation, let alone progress.

An environment where ideas are welcomed does not judge them by their provenance. It sounds like a peculiar idea that somehow deviancy is a good thing. The word itself though is pejorative. It suggests that different is wrong and similarity is right. Neither is wrong nor right. It is a judgement.

Leaders extend their parenthesis by listening to the minority. They deepen their support by listening to the majority. When the leader signals an interest in minorities, they signal interest in the future.

The emotional difference of new

The incumbency is logical and familiar. 'Old' is tried and tested. This is where the majority is – normality. Novelty, on the other hand, is always emotional. It creates interest and excitement but also fear of the unknown. This is why the adjective 'new' is used so frequently as a way of attracting attention.

The motto of the US is *E pluribus unum*, out of the many (or the minorities) comes one. This could be very much the reason why new ideas are more easily assimilated in the US.

The power of these small minority groups has been seen with both Extinction Rebellion and the Brexit Party in the UK and the Tea Party in the US. It may well be that to many of Donald Trump's supporters, he represented (what was perceived as, at least) the minority point of view. In creating a liberal consensus in the media, it may well be that this was what caused the rebellion.

When these minorities have no hope of representation, they can lose faith in participating in the process. For this reason, turnout in the 2020 elections in the US may be very low. The turnout for the UK election in 2019 was the fifth lowest in 100 years.

The same applies in teams. When some feel they have no representation with a leader, then the team starts to fall apart in terms of cohesion. This is why the leader has to stay in touch with minority views.

Minority views as news

This idea of the minority also applies to news because all news stories represent a minority – the psychology of the unexpected. If it happens all the time, it's not a story. 'Dog bites man' is the majority. 'Man bites dog' is the minority. This creates the warped view often depicted by media.

It's no accident that, for instance, both Boris Johnson and President Trump were known TV personalities before winning the highest leadership roles in politics.

Could it be though that minority stories have now become so powerful that news dictates the outcome? For instance, Donald Trump's presidential campaign was the story the media wanted because it would attract more viewers. The minority story represents more mystery and therefore adds more value.

Acceptance of the quantum superposition

One of the key aspects of Infinite Leadership that is difficult to grasp is the notion that leaders can move quickly between extremes. If we take analytical thinking, for instance. Juxtaposing between drill-down and look-across may sound difficult, but with practice it becomes easier. How do we know this? Because the extremes always need to be trained. We develop basic intelligence in schools and universities to allow the development of Western reductionism. We train mindfulness and contemplation in every religion. These all benefit from practice. So why can't we have a new infinity discipline that teaches the ability to juxtapose?

If we want to develop real capacity, it's important to concentrate on how we use our time. This doesn't mean that we should be working all the time to develop capacity. We know that's not how capacity is developed. You can't have a powerful out breath unless you develop the power of the in breath. Leadership performance is similar. If we're going to aspire to balance, then we need to consider the effects that leadership has on us. Is it reasonable for you to work eighteen hours a day, seven days a week? What would you feel about an employer that made you do those hours? You'd probably object, so when you're the leader, you have to regulate yourself. You have to take responsibility.

If you want the ultimate in performance in terms of concentrated focus and intense activity, then you need to develop the capacity for the opposite. This is not just rest. For some, it's intensive rest. It means that when you're not working you need to be doing something that demands your full attention. This is why so many business leaders are extreme sports devotees, for instance.

But this doesn't necessarily fit everyone and even if it did, it would not be sustainable into middle age. This means that at some point, you will need to master total relaxation. For some, this means actively and deliberately learning how to do nothing. This can come with meditation, but it can also happen in a variety of activities.

Many will spend their time in pursuit of a new management model. The only ones that will work long term are the ones that involve balance. To perform at the highest level requires focus and concentration. To do this for decades requires another gift. The ability to do nothing.

This might seem an odd idea for a high achiever. When you're doing nothing, your body is repairing, organizing your thoughts and replenishing burnt energy. Never forget that when you're doing nothing, you're doing a great deal.

Never forget that when you're doing nothing, you're doing a great deal.

This is also about your ability to trust yourself. It takes time to create a vision. If it comes at all, then it usually evolves once you discuss it. Furthermore, you don't create just one vision. Each problem encountered needs a vision of how it can be dealt with positively.

Stressed leaders are, of course, unbalanced. Stress creates a temporary sense of lost coordinates. To recreate these, leaders can sometimes fall back into old patterns of behaviour to cope. This ends up with progress and time being lost. It can also cost relationships. This is why time spent reframing problems can be invaluable. It can feel like moving slowly, but in the longer term, it allows faster movement. A good way of reframing this is to explain a problem to a colleague and ask for their opinion. This is when the four most powerful words in leadership can be deployed: 'What do you think?' This is not an indicator of confusion in a leader, but an invitation for a colleague to speak.

Leaders sometimes find themselves under stress, wanting to solve every problem themselves and not realizing that they are contributing to them. This is why the leader's self-awareness really matters. Sometimes the world can close in and the leader can feel as if they're completely on their own. This is when they need to be their own best friend and step away for some perspective.

All leaders make mistakes, but it's how they are made that matters. If something fails in a genuine attempt to try to do something new, then that's forgivable. Making the same mistakes as a result of repeating patterns of behaviour is less so. Recognizing these patterns is key and can be embedded into 360-degree appraisals.

In the same way that all big accidents are usually caused by a string of small things going wrong, just about all management failure has an element of imbalance. The clues to this are all around. Imbalance happens first in the leader themselves. Either they are pursuing the wrong things or they're being distracted and not paying enough attention. The leader cannot spot imbalance in other leaders if they can't spot it in themselves. This is why they need to spend time thinking carefully about the organization. They can't do that when they are going at warp speed.

Leaders get into their position by being successful in one area. They stay there with other means. They stay by having the imagination and perspective to keep checking. All good leaders have the ability to use anxiety creatively.

This means that the leader needs to be constantly reinventing different ways of measuring balance against a range of scales:

Local – Global
Male – Female
Tactical – Strategic
Short-term – Long-term
Me – We
Home – Work
Execution – Thinking
Static – Mobile
Personal – Organizational
Young – Old
Homogenous – Diverse
Natural – Artificial
Today – Tomorrow

Scott Stephenson writing in *Forbes*[10] magazine summed it up:

> Good management is the disciplined and planned approach to organizing activities, making sure that work is consistent and aligned to produce the desired results. There's a good understanding on the part of the people inside the operation of what's needed and wanted and how the work is going to proceed. And it's all done with a view of resource requirements today and into the future so that there's a planned approach to ensure operations can be sustained and supported for years to come. That's good management, and that's what produces results in any particular period of time.

In contrast, leadership is not only about optimizing what we have today. It's also about maximizing the potential of the organization over a longer period of time. It's about making sure that the core value proposition and commitments of the business are solidly grounded. It's thinking hard about the interaction of the core capabilities of the enterprise and what's needed and wanted in the world – and how to bring those things together. It's helping people grow and influencing what matters and what should receive attention. It's culture setting. Ultimately, it's about defining what is valued.

A world of mixed realities

It was the Irish poet W B Yeats that said: 'The world is full of magic things, patiently waiting for our senses to grow sharper.'[11] The leader's job is to be perceptive, to notice. It's difficult to do this if the leader is self-obsessed. It takes time and skill to listen to people and to notice things. It is possible to be highly educated yet not see signs that are front and centre. This is difficult because there are multiple realities to perceive.

What do we mean by this? Every time the leader spends time talking to staff, customers, shareholders, cleaners, bankers, each is encountering a different reality. A good yardstick is to try to imagine ten other realities or perspectives each day. All of this deepens the leader's field of perception. It allows a better understanding of what is required.

The problem for leaders is that reality is changed and rearranged by status. The ability to see things that are not there and derive value. Part of the leader's job is to understand the magic of leadership. This is not from an egocentric point of view – quite the contrary. It is to be able to use it positively and to recognize that both praise and criticism from leadership are amplified and therefore must be used carefully. Power is there to create utility, not authority.

> *The problem for leaders is that reality is changed and rearranged by status.*

It may be that some colleagues are nervous around authority. Sometimes, those in authority like the feeling of power this gives them. But although this is a definite reality for subordinates, the leader must ask: 'What is it we are trying to achieve together?' If the leader is just trying to make money, then that's not leadership. Money is always the by-product of a successful culture. To concentrate on the end goal alone is to miss the point of what makes wealth. It has to be created from sustainable sources for it to be truly enduring.

The leader as a bringer of light

Leaders can use the power and the attention they generate to benefit colleagues. When leaders praise individuals it can unleash tremendous power. This is the power of conviction. It costs the leader nothing to apply it, but it does require them to be thinking about how they can use their position to motivate others.

In this respect, leaders can have a Promethean effect, by bringing warmth and illuminating the darkness. That's why it's important that they can converse with people at all levels of the organization. What difference does it make if the area around you is illuminated? First, it helps to orientate the person. Suddenly, the context of what they do is made legitimate because it's recognized by others. The leader's attention allows the colleague to locate themselves. This is as true emotionally as it is organizationally. Great leaders have the ability to alter realities and deepen fields of perception. This allows colleagues to create their own map. The map after all is not a territory but is a representation of reality, just like leadership. It's no accident that when people say 'I'm lost' it's an emotional as well as a factual statement.

Incidentally, this orientation is as much to the leader's benefit as it is to the rest of the team. There are many leaders whose mental states have been worsened by the isolation following their success, eg Howard Hughes, Randolph Hearst, Michael Jackson.

The leader's interpretation of history is also a key part of this. In *Nineteen Eighty-Four*, George Orwell writes:

> 'Who controls the past,' ran the Party slogan, 'controls the future: who controls the present controls the past.'[12]

To illustrate the meaning of this quote, the protagonist Winston Smith uses the example that Oceania is at war with Eurasia. While the Party claims that Oceania has always been at war with Eurasia, Winston can clearly remember a time, four years ago, when Oceania and Eurasia were in alliance. This knowledge, however, exists only in his 'own consciousness' because the Party has rewritten history so that this alliance never happened.

It is this manipulation of the truth, or 'reality control' as Winston calls it, that contributes to the Party's everlasting and totalitarian power. It can make people believe whatever it tells them because it rewrites history accordingly.

It is also worth noting the text from Emmanuel Goldstein, who is the principal enemy of the state according to the Party of the totalitarian Oceania. Goldstein's book further explains the Party's control of the past:

> The past is whatever the records and the memories agree upon. And since the Party is in full control of all records and in equally

full control of the minds of its members, it follows that the past is whatever the Party chooses to make it.

Our collective past is now held on social media. If it cannot be found there, it may never have happened. This is why the team is so important; the recollection of memories and shared experiences in the team is fundamental to the existence of the culture.

Leadership coaching

There are plenty of leadership coaches out there, but the most important voice you're hearing now is you. The leader's relationship with everyone is firstly dictated by the dialogue they have with themselves.

You can enhance leadership ability but, by its very nature, not all the greatest challenges of leadership can be taught institutionally. It can be fully completed only by autodidacticism and this is not a finite process. Long term, the leader's most important relationship is with themselves.

Understanding the importance of liminal states

A liminal state is the quality of ambiguity or disorientation or freedom that occurs in-between states. Being present in one world only tends to encourage the Western reductionist analytical state. Moving between states has always been recognized as a mysterious moment. It is recognized at birth, death, marriage, coming of age, etc. Passing over water from one end of a bridge to another was recognized by Romans who made a votive offering to the river below.[13]

This is a good state for leaders to practise – to occupy the space between customer and supplier, or employee and management, or investor and company. This requires that the leader moves out of the comfort zone that surrounds them.

Daydreaming

The last thing you would associate with dynamic leadership is daydreaming, but this too is an important aspect of the zero state.

In a piece entitled 'The creativity of the wandering mind',[14] Tom Jacobs writing in *Pacific Standard* magazine said: 'Mindless tasks that allow our thoughts to roam can be catalysts for innovation.' He was describing the work of Benjamin Baird and Jonathan Schooler of the University of California, Santa Barbara's META Lab (which focuses on memory, emotion, thought and awareness).

Baird and his colleagues experimented on 135 people, aged 19 to 35. Their creativity was measured by performance on the classic Unusual Uses task. This is where each participant is given two minutes to come up with as many uses as possible for a specific item, such as a brick. Besides the sheer number of responses, their answers are judged on originality, flexibility and level of detail.

All the participants began by tackling two such problems. One-quarter of them then spent 12 minutes on an intellectually demanding task, which demanded constant attention. Another quarter spent that same amount of time on an undemanding task, which only required them to provide 'infrequent responses'. Another quarter was instructed to rest for 12 minutes, while the rest went directly to the next task without a break.

All then tackled four additional rounds of the Unusual Uses task. Two were repeats of the tests they had performed earlier, and two featured objects that were new to them.

Those who had performed the undemanding task in the interim had significantly higher scores than those in any of the other categories (including the people who had simply rested for 12 minutes). However, this jump in creativity occurred only for the items they were tackling for a second time. They did not score any better than the others when presented with a new object.

This suggests their creative solutions 'resulted from an incubation process', which was 'characterized by high levels of mind wandering', said the researchers. Having had a chance to mull over the first two objects they were presented with (thanks to the relatively mindless task they performed in the interim), they came up with more creative ideas when given the opportunity to revisit them.

The researchers can't be sure why, but they point to neuroimaging studies that suggest that while the mind is wandering, several different brain networks interact. They speculate that this 'relatively rare' state may enhance creative thinking.

But why did those stuck with a boring task do better than those who had simply rested for 12 minutes? It's impossible to say for certain, but being free to think about anything, their minds presumably drifted somewhere else entirely – perhaps to a pleasant (or challenging) subject that occupied their entire attention.

The implication here is interesting. We can't prove this scientifically, but what if the difference between work-based thinking and daydreaming revolves around free will? This would suggest the brain is more creative when allowed to wander rather than being singularly focused on narrow and consciously driven Western reductionism. Rather than forcing our minds down the classic analytical route, if there's an allowance and trust in the mind, alternative solutions become so much more accessible. Neither system is better, the ideal solution is a balance of both.

Hypnagogia

It may be that this wandering state is more common than we think. There is a zone, between waking and sleep, when consciousness begins to warp. We pass through this boundary twice a day, sometimes more. On each occasion we seek to hurry through the transition, anxious to complete the procedure. Seldom do we consciously attempt to use this transition productively. Rigid reductionist thinking starts to dissolve into daydreaming. Known as the hypnagogic state, it has received only sporadic attention from researchers over the years, but a recent series of studies has renewed interest in this twilight period, with the hope it can reveal something fundamental about consciousness itself.

Dr Valdas Noreika is a researcher in neuroscience at Cambridge University. He's been looking into linguistic intrusions, ie the sudden emergence of unpredictable anomalies in the stream of inner speech during the transition from a relaxed to a drowsy state of mind. This is often accompanied by hypnagogic experiences, most commonly a change in perceptual imagery. This is illustrated scientifically by the activity in the different parts of the brain as measured by EEGs.

Basically, he reports that in the drowsy state, the hemispheres of the brain connect together more randomly and unexpectedly in a similar way to the effects of LSD.

Writing in *The Lancet*[15] in April 2018, Adam Powell said:

In the course of western thought, dualities have been highly influential, pitting mind and soul against brain and body, the act of sensing against the act of perceiving, sanity against insanity, hallucinations and delusions against truth and reality. Indeed, even today, common theories of psychosis discuss causes and consequences in terms of reality monitoring: some have it; some do not. These notions span back quite far – not least, to Aristotelian theories of perception – and owe a great deal to European philosophers, such as Michel de Montaigne, Thomas Hobbes, and René Descartes.

Powell points out that Descartes crystallized the dualism of the individual, which led philosophers to locate personal identity in the 'continuous mind rather than the fleeting body'. For figures such as theologian Joseph Butler and philosopher/physician John Locke, identity was interior. But what of the interior–exterior divide? Could the mind deceive the senses, or vice versa? This is apparent in the waking versus sleeping liminal state.

In his essay 'Optics',[16] for example, Descartes recognized that artistic depictions of circles are often formed by ovals, where the mind sees an object via an image that does not perfectly resemble it. Indeed the eye sees an image that is inverted and the brain interprets it.

But this deals only with when the individual is awake or asleep. As psychiatric medicine developed, another possibility was introduced. French psychiatrists such as Alfred Maury[17] highlighted the fecundity of hypnagogia. In fact, Maury coined the phrase 'hypnagogic hallucinations' as early as 1848, as a way of clustering the visual, auditory, haptic and emotional phenomena accompanying the transition between waking and sleeping.

Powell says that more than a third of the population reports having these experiences. So it's worth a try. It would stand to reason that any suspension or dilution of the Western reductionist state must result in an alternative process. This may be more what might be known as 'free association' – a distinct process in psychoanalytic therapy.

Traditionally, the hypnagogic state has been studied as part of narcolepsy, where the brain's inability to separate waking life and dreaming can result in hallucinations. But it's also part of the normal transition into sleep, beginning when the mind is first affected by drowsiness and ending with the loss of consciousness. It's brief and often slips by unnoticed, but consistent careful attention to the inner experience as you fall asleep can reveal curious sounds, abstract scenery and tumbling thoughts.

Training for ambiguity

The range of experimental techniques illustrates not just the breadth of alternative processes but also the narrowness of institutional training. The reflex response to so much of this 'illegitimate' thinking is to reject it. This is unsurprising because training for logical analysis is designed to exclude what appears at first to be illogical. The myth is that logic is serious work and that play is not when the two are part of the same process. When logic is all you've got, it's actually really quite a handicap. You can only deal in one reality, when balanced leadership retains awareness of different consciousness levels and realities.

This is one of the great signs of mediocrity. Certainty is a middle management idea. Leaders have to commune with ambiguity, so let's start training them and ourselves for that. We could term this to be part of our personal 'hourglass'. First, we learn the reductionist method, then we learn that it's not the whole story and that we have not yet completed our education, because we never do. The myth of the institutional rubric is that when the qualification is achieved, the legitimate learning ends, too.

Summary

The zero state creates huge opportunities, both from being balanced and understanding the importance of the liminal state that exists between two extremes. We can have different levels of balance at different levels of leadership. We can also change around the axes on the model to understand balance in one continuum versus another. In reality, this is beginning to get closer to the real challenge of leadership. This is not to be balanced on just two axes, but multiple ones. This makes leadership look like a child's toy – a sphere with multiple channels where the leader needs to keep the ball centred across all of them simultaneously.

Leadership can be seen in many different ways. It also exists in many different ways, constantly changing its position to examine a situation from multiple contexts. The infinite task is not just to stay balanced, but to be ready to deploy to the extremes quickly and flexibly.

There is a huge benefit to residing at the infinite zero point. It is the closest point to deploy to any extreme. Next, we explore how this can be applied to a new type of economic activity and how it compares to what we have currently.

CHAPTER SIX

Zeronomics

How do the models affect our understanding of economics? Could they be used to explain the success or failure of start-ups? How successful is current investment thinking? Does it promote more or less balance within companies and leadership teams? What are the implications of this failure? How can it be that this system of capital destroys the majority of companies that it touches, yet is still deemed to be the least worst? Is that what we mean by balanced? How will this change as a result of the pandemic?

The holy grail of every national economy is for it to be balanced. Governments spend a great deal of time trying to balance an economy or trying to tilt it marginally in one direction or another.

It does feel as if the economy is out of balance, regardless of what happens to be going on at any given moment. Sometimes it's whipped into a frenzy of jittery growth and uncomfortably high asset prices. But we don't readily accept record low unemployment and record high stock market prices. Instead, we tend to believe that these positive data points portend doom. And yet, people feel embarrassed to have missed the party whenever the markets go up and often end up buying assets at high prices in spite of their reservations. Sometimes the economy menaces with the threat of crises, recessions and imminent collapse. Hardly anyone says, 'What a great time to invest in the future.' Instead, convinced that worse is to come, we find ourselves selling low, hoping to cash out before the catastrophe drives the economy to hit rock bottom.

Meanwhile, our policymaking leaders tinker with their tools and safety valves, trying to nudge the economy back into balance either way by deploying monetary and fiscal policy, interest rates, tax incentives and even through moral exhortations. We don't have much confidence in policymakers and economists these days, though. Nor does anyone believe anymore that the economy is a self-correcting balancing mechanism. No one believes in the 'Rational Man' who used to underpin its workings. He appears to have been transformed into 'Irrational Man'. Why? If fear is the natural resting state that governs our view of the economy, then we will always tend to look for a superhero, a single person, a saviour who can miraculously rescue us from the seemingly random vicissitudes of the world economy. We want to be saved before the dysrhythmia of the economy gives us a heart attack. It seems we now take imbalance as the new steady state.

Imbalance misses opportunity

There is a readily identifiable *superhero*, but it's not who you think. It is not the person to whom we are allocating capital and savings. It is not the person on the covers of business magazines or on the front pages of the major papers. The single most adept person at efficiently marshalling resources, often without access to capital, networks, resources, education or external support, happens now to be the fastest growing category of entrepreneurial business leaders in the US – it's a woman, and especially a woman of colour. According to a report commissioned by American Express,[1] while the number of female-owned businesses grew by 58 per cent from 2007 to 2018, the number of firms in the US owned by black women grew by 164 per cent. There were 2.4 million African American women-owned businesses in 2018, and most were owned by women aged 35 to 54. According to the Federal Reserve Bank of Kansas, black women are the only racial or ethnic group with more business ownership than their male peers.[2]

Most investors, such as venture capital and private equity firms, are looking but sadly do not seem to find her. They should be, but they cannot seem to find her. CrunchBase news reported that 77.1 per cent of founders who received VC (venture capital) 'were white – regardless of gender and education'; 1 per cent were black. Female founders got just 9 per cent of their capital, Latino founders got 1.8 per cent and Asians got 17.7 per cent.[3] What is the problem?

Black women are the only racial or ethnic group with more business ownership than their male peers.

Investors often say that they don't invest in businesses. They invest in people. What they mean by this is very specific. They invest in people who have the vision to see a business become a fast-growing, highly profitable investment, known as a 'unicorn' in the industry. They are looking to invest in businesses that will reach a $1 billion valuation within a few years. It requires many skill sets to move a business from the basement or the dining room table to unicorn status. Investors look for business leaders who already have these skills and the networks of friends and businesses that can help them scale. If you went to business school, it is more likely that you are part of a network like this. But most black female entrepreneurs did not go to business school.

Generally, the black female running a little business is not even considered to be a start-up – she's just hardscrabble. No matter that she is more efficient. If she is not perceived to be running a scalable business, then institutions will not invest.

Scaling is a very specific skill set, which involves gathering distribution partners. These are not friends who help with sales. These are large organizations that have known brand names. It involves the acquisition of negotiating power so that one can cut the cost of inputs. It involves legal skills that allow the business to protect itself against intellectual property theft and competition from departed employees. It is hard to find all these skills in a single person. Most people have a network of experts, often friends across other industries, that they can turn to for advice and assistance. Our superhero often has none of these advantages.

Imbalance creates waste

No investor is looking for slow, steady conservatism or for a 'balanced' long-term entrepreneur. They want high-growth, high-profit unicorns and they want lots of them. A unicorn is a firm that achieves a valuation of $1 billion in a matter of a few years. These days it is no longer enough to make a 10× per cent return. Investors want 10 times their money back. It's not that this is easy to achieve. Most don't get anywhere even close. If we look at companies that have gone public through an initial public offering (IPO), we see that more than half the IPOs between 1975 and 2011 had negative returns after their first five years of trading.[4] From 1980 to 2016 the average six-month return was 6 per cent. So, many are unicorn hunting, few are bringing any home.

It also matters when you buy a unicorn. It's no use buying shares in Amazon after they are worth x per share but before they hit an all-time high of y per share. The idea is to find an Amazon or an Apple or an Uber when they are still just a person with an idea in a basement or a garage. This is how investors make 10× or more. This stage of investing is called seed capital. It's seriously risky. Most such ventures fail. But, at the seed stage, presumably the black female founder is on an even footing with her peer competitors. Yet still this superhero does not attract the capital. So, who gets it?

Not the one driven by imperative. Investors choose the one who is driven by ego. They are drawn to the person who convincingly argues that they are going to be the next Uber, Apple or Stripe. They back the ones with the personal connections and networks that would permit them to scale the business. But, the ecosystem of private capital is mainly orientated towards the unicorn that flies rather than the solid workhorse that a sole-trading entrepreneur represents. The system leans towards those who most delightfully confection and embellish the story and leans away from those whose story is rooted in the dreary facts of cash flow and actual sales. This explains how some high-profile failures have occurred. Some of the best storytellers turn out to be liars. This is what happened at Theranos, the blood testing firm that charged clients for technology that it knew did not work.

Imbalance creates more imbalance

All these reasons help explain why early stage private investors backed Adam Neumann. The founder of WeWork had all the requisite characteristics we like to look for in a superhero leader. *The New York Times* wrote he had 'an inexplicably persuasive charisma and a taste for risk'[5] and

> ... an uncanny ability to read people, from potential investors to reporters, gain their loyalty and then sell them on his vision of a 'capitalist kibbutz' on a global scale. He benefited from a frenetic, nonstop energy, and silly as it may sound, there's no question that Mr. Neumann's good hair and looks helped his cause. At 6'5", he had a physical presence that could dominate a room.

He had married into a Hollywood family. His sister had been Miss Israel. He was also very young, just 30 when he launched WeWork. The WeWork parties were also really good. There were even parties on bad days. He is said to have handed out vodka shots after rounds of employee firings.

His vision was immense. He raised $8.4 billion and achieved a theoretical valuation of $47 billion, even though the firm never made a profit. All looked fine until the real financial scrutiny began in the run-up to the planned flotation of the firm's shares on public stock markets. The initial public offering had to be shelved when investors questioned the valuation, especially given that the firm had lost a billion dollars every year for the previous three years. Still, private investors had bought into his vision, which had been supported by Goldman Sachs, which led the fundraising round. As *The New Yorker* put it, 'The company's proposition was as intoxicating as it was vague.'[6] What was the vision? Neumann offered the world a convivial place to work, complete with brightly coloured furniture, cool parties and a new work ethos that included not eating meat.

As often happens with leaders, what they do and who they are start to conflict. His authenticity became suspect when he announced that the firm would not underwrite the cost of staff meals that included meat, nor would he permit meat to be offered at the WeWork sites. Yet, he remained a meat eater himself, often eating meat in front of colleagues while inside his office. It also became clear that he was double dealing on a far more serious level, selling his own shares to employees without declaring it and selling assets to the firm that ought to have belonged to the firm in the first place, like the 'We' trademark, for which he received (and later returned) $5.9 million. These sins seemed more egregious to most than the one that seems to have finally brought him down. Had he not left a sizeable amount of marijuana in a cereal box on a friend's Gulfstream G650 private jet, which the crew discovered upon landing in Israel, he might still be running the firm.

In all, the various revelations and loss of confidence caused the firm to lose $39 billion in a single year. In the end, the biggest backer of the firm, SoftBank, had to throw in $2 billion to prevent the firm's outright collapse. Neumann resigned but was still entitled to another $2 billion or so based on his contract. It may yet be found that the business was great but the founder's leadership of it was poor. Or it may be that the business model itself was wrong, but it seems less likely. After all, other similar firms in the property business with similar business models, like Regus, had been making real money. The real question is why did Neumann attract so much interest and investment compared with them?

There are many theories about what drives investors. Bloomberg's Emily Chang described one part of the VC ecosystem in Silicon Valley as a 'Brotopia'.[7] The idea was that investments followed those start-ups that supplied what *Vanity Fair* called the best 'drug-heavy, sex-heavy' parties.[8] This part of the ecosystem was making investment decisions for reasons that seem to have had little to do with financial returns. Another theory is that venture capitalists have become so focused on software that they won't invest in anything real or which involves bricks and mortar, because that's not efficient.

But more efficient for who? Does it help a community if a firm has no physical presence within it? Does it matter? It certainly does when that community believes it doesn't pay its fair share of taxes to help the community stay balanced.

This may be another filter that keeps women and minorities out of the ecosystem. The typical minority or female start-up is not a software play because most women are not coders. The National Science Foundation says that less than 17 per cent of computer science majors are female.[9] One software engineer at Google, James Damore, achieved brief fame for an 'anti-diversity' memo,[10] in which he suggested that the few female coders at Google were only there for reasons of political correctness. In other words, even the women who make it into the software engineering club are not very welcome, even in Silicon Valley. So, if women aren't making software and that's all the investors want, then we see another reason why there is a mismatch.

Resource conservation

But there is a bigger question. How is it that we are ever more careful about how we deploy every kind of resource except money? People are turning the lights off and dialling down the air conditioning. They are increasingly replacing their loud gasoline guzzlers with quiet electric vehicles. New clothes are no longer 'in'. People are preferring to repurpose second-hand clothes in order to conserve resources. More and more we are eating less and less meat. Yet, few seem to ask how efficient our leaders are with resources, especially with the one resource that we seem to think is most important in business – capital.

Wasting money is perhaps inherent in the investment process. The professional investment community expects to lose money. They expect to lose a lot of money. The idea is that only one out of ten investments will really pay off. Two or three will do fine. The rest will fail. It's a high-risk, high-return business. The institutional and private investors are not in it for social reasons. Their aim is not to better the community. The need is to achieve at least a 3× return overall in order to justify the fees that they charge and to cover their overheads. A return of less than 12 per cent isn't sufficient to warrant the risk. No one in the VC world sets out to back a business that is going to fail. They only choose winners. Still, many of the firms they back fail. *Most* fail. TechCrunch found that 96 per cent of all start-ups backed by venture capitalists were 'juggling somewhere between breaking even and downright losing money (remember to adjust for inflation)'.[11]

To be clear, just because WeWork didn't work doesn't mean nothing in the ecosystem works. Beyond Meat, which makes vegan and vegetarian meat substitutes, had a spectacular IPO the same year that WeWork failed. The share price rose 734 per cent after the IPO launched. It was possible to see the difference between the two firms simply by looking at how efficiently they deployed capital. CNBC Disruptor 50 published

FIGURE 6.1 VC funds – return on investment

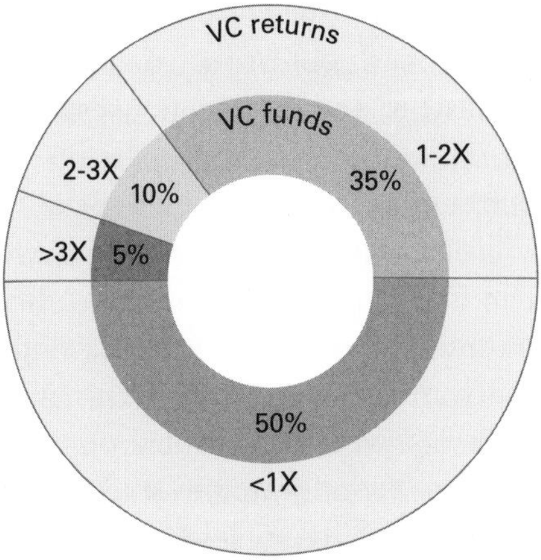

Source: Money Talks, Gil Ben-Artzy, UpWest Labs, LinkedIn SlideShare, https://www.slideshare.
net/gilbenartzy/money-talks-things-you-learn-after-77-investment-rounds (archived at https://
perma.cc/L28K-UH24)

an insightful analysis of WeWork by the CEO of FCLTGlobal, Sarah Williamson, and MD Bhakti Mirchandani in December 2019, which compared WeWork with Beyond Meat, Uber and Lyft. In short, WeWork's costs were out of control. They said, 'The difference between capital raised and spent, normalized for assets, has great predictive value. Compared to the other companies here, they (WeWork) were losing more money while raising less capital, relative to their assets.'[12]

Note that Uber was another firm that became a unicorn in spite of allegations of improprieties, which included insider trading, surge pricing incidents that gouged clients unexpectedly when disasters were occurring, attacks by drivers on customers and the fact that the CEO called the firm 'Boober' apparently in reference to its female passengers. Who knows how much value was lost due to Uber's cavalier approach. In a world that is prepared to give so much money to a young entrepreneur, character matters after all. Is the capital something the person has stewardship of? Or does that much money give the entrepreneur the feeling that they have the right to rip cash out of the company for personal gains? This is a persistent and haunting question for many investors.

This is a social question as well. After all, most of the net new jobs are created by little companies that employ fewer than 50 people. In the US, in 2019 the Small Business Administration said the 30.7 million small businesses in America employed 47.3 per cent of the total private workforce.[13] So it is striking that our collective pools of savings, whether personal or in the form of pensions, generally do not get allocated to start-ups. We entrust these funds to the professional investing institutions, and they do not allocate the capital here either. This is because these investments are risky. It is because they don't generate big enough returns for professional investors. It is because it is a lot of work to sift through the many firms that may be making money but are not scalable. Size matters. Bigger is better. Investors seek scalability. This presents an interesting social problem.

How many small businesses could be scaled but aren't because the leader running them doesn't have the core skills or the network of expertise to help them do this? How many other firms could have been as scalable as WeWork, but did not attract the capital because their leaders were not as readily identifiable as leadership material as Adam Neumann? Are there entrepreneurial leaders who could help the economy grow and spur innovation but who the markets ignore? Possibly so. How is this possible in a world where almost every economy is more capitalistic than before? Even China has adopted a progressive form of capitalism. Could it be that the market is failing to find profit opportunities because investors are so enamoured of a certain familiar type of leader? Is it because we lack confidence in the people who don't look or act the way we think a leader should?

What we look for

We should think about what we look for in a leader. This might help explain why we keep choosing poor business leaders. For example, we are enamoured of height – tall people and tall buildings, tall tales and high places. Earlier we mentioned that human height confers leadership qualities on a person. It confers them on a business too. Size is similar to height in this respect. Think about the tendency for corporate headquarters to be very tall. Height and vision seem interconnected. The higher a business flies, the more attractive it seems to be. Tall buildings have been a symbol of success, even though the tallest buildings are often seen as a precursor to a slowdown or recession. Today we see start-ups that are reaching for the stars, like Elon Musk's SpaceX and Richard Branson's Virgin Galactic. We want to buy a place in space because only God lives there, high up above Mount Olympus. It's hard to overlook the simple fact that the folks with capital like to create phallic symbols on the skyline.

One of the most renowned unicorns is Apple. Interestingly, Steve Jobs wasn't able to raise venture capital money either. In one video he says that one VC investor called him a 'renegade from the human race' because 'I had longer hair then'.[14] It is interesting to note that Apple chose the shape of a ring, a circle, a zero for its headquarters and has ended up with a higher degree of public trust than its competitors. Dr Paul Marsden of the University of the Arts London is a consumer psychologist who sums it up nicely: 'The psychology of trust – whether it's a human, brand or app – is based on two dimensions: competence and intention, can they help, and do they care enough to want to help?'[15] The Apple ring is a visible symbol of organic growth and self-support. It is a portal to infinite possibilities. It is not like the phallic symbol we see at SpaceX's headquarters.

Imbalance drives us in the opposite direction

Fear drives us towards a leader who looks like a saviour. If we assume that the world economy is inevitably listing towards disaster, like a torpedoed ship, then we need a rescuer. If we cannot recognize or acknowledge when the economy is a success, then we never feel good enough to take the risks that are required to generate new growth from new kinds of businesses. So we need to rebalance how we think about the economy. We need to think about ergonomics, the process of balancing economic possibility and financial risk but with a view to achieving more ubiquity and less scarcity. But how is this possible? Can we really create something out of nothing? How can we learn to envisage ubiquity in a world dominated by scarcity?

First, the ship we call the world economy is not necessarily torpedoed or listing. In fact, as many authors have eloquently explained, the world economy keeps delivering ever better outcomes. One thinks of Stephen Pinker, who showed how dramatically the problems of poverty and disease have been radically improved since the 18th century.[16] *Abundance* by Peter Diamandis and Steven Kotler[17] drew a convincing picture of a world in which technology consistently permits us to do more and more with less and less. Hans Rosling with his son Ola Rosling and daughter-in-law Anna Rosling Rönnlund showed us in their book *Factfulness*[18] that most people are both absolutely and relatively better off than ever before, by almost every metric from life expectancy to income.

The real trouble begins with the first cardinal assumption that underpins modern economics, which is scarcity. There isn't enough. There will never be enough. Of anything. So, economics as a science is largely a scramble for diminishing and scarce resources. As prices rise and populations grow, we also denude the planet of its most valuable resources including food, water, energy and, arguably, goodwill. Everyone knows that prices are established from the trade-off between supply and demand. It was Thomas Malthus who firmly rooted us in this mindset back in 1798 when he argued that the growth of food was linear and limited while population growth could be exponential. So, the more food, the more people. Eventually there would be too many people, more than the food supply could support. Malthusians have been trying to control population growth ever since. As a result of this scarcity mindset, the Scottish writer Thomas Carlyle slapped a label on the economics profession, calling it 'the dismal science'.[19] Carlyle was another Renaissance man – a historian, satirist, philosopher, translator, mathematician and teacher.

The dismal science provokes fear partly because the economy demands that we keep up with constant change. It provokes fear because it is the source of new inventions and processes that we don't understand. How many of us fear technology just because we can't keep up with it? This is not a new phenomenon.

To rebalance our leadership, we need an almost existential approach to everything. This is where 'What if?' thinking comes in. What if we were going to start from a blank sheet of paper? What if we were just starting up? How would we do this? Supposing we didn't have this budget, what level of budget would be needed (zero-based budgeting)?

Zero-state thinking doesn't require capital. It can use its 'convening' power to bring resources together. It identifies alignments and mutuality to create narratives around benefits. Let's begin by looking at the effects that intersecting trends have had on economic thinking.

Decapitalization

The relationship between the cost of technology and its power has been inverse for 50 years. As a result of Moore's Law,[20] technology has doubled in power every two years. As it has, the cost of that technology has fallen to the extent that the huge capacities needed to process information have become virtually free.

In just about every tertiary service-based industry, the level of capital required has diminished to vanishing point. When private equity is applied to start-ups, in most instances the only provision is for working capital. How long does it take from start-up to invoice payment in a tertiary environment? Let's say six months, maximum. If those starting up cannot lower outgoings or save enough for six months or finance an overdraft, then will they be disciplined enough to be long-term entrepreneurs? The vast majority of new business startups fail.[21] In a study of more than 2,000 venture-backed start-ups using $1 million or more of capital, nearly half of the investors lost all their money.

This is all the more curious when you consider that many of the lenders that provide capital are highly experienced entrepreneurs themselves. How can it be that so many leaders fail when surrounded by so much experience? This is by no means an outlier in terms of failure. Another survey puts the failure rate at 80 per cent.[22]

The scale of the waste is staggering, yet it is a model that persists. Why? Partially because there's been no impetus to do better. The other factor is because tax losses in one play can be used to improve performance in another. So for instance, if investment in Company A produces massive losses, the co-investors in that business may lose their money but the one with the 'tag and drag' rights over shareholders can then use the tax losses. This then increases the amount of reinvestment that can be made in the successful company at the expense of other players.

This creates a sort of centripetal effect around only the most successful companies in the portfolio and these, of course, become very, very successful, powered effectively by the failure of the others.

There's no interest from private equity in companies that cannot offer spectacular growth. They want unicorns not dray horses. And therein lies the problem. What is the purpose of capital investment? Is it to reward cautious, consistent, caring leadership or is it to make a large amount of money in the short term? You don't have to answer that because the answer is obvious. This is not about economic rationalism.

As one person, who had just been in front of private equity investors, put it: 'What they want to hear is insanity. They want leadership with no destination.' This is an interesting point because it suggests that this journey without destination is what investors want. In many respects, then, the capital message is similar to the political message – we're perpetually on a track to a better future.

The reason we have such poor leadership is because that's exactly what we want. For the failure rate to be so high, there must be other criteria at play.

Imbalance causes business failure

There are lots of thoroughly good reasons for why a business fails. At the heart of it though is leadership failure. And some of this is very basic. To beat the 75 per cent failure rate all a business needs to do is to get its expenses lower than its revenues. This is the first test of leadership. It sounds stupid and basic, but if a company does this, then it survives. But why doesn't it?

Hubris

Much entrepreneurship, especially later in life, is based on ambition or an idea. Nothing wrong with that. But the congratulations invariably come to entrepreneurs on the announcement that they are starting up, not when they have completed their first three years.

There is an expectation that rewards should flow as a result of having assembled the launch proposition. The phrase 'serial entrepreneur' often embodies this. It is not enough to create businesses that fail or underperform as some indicator of leadership ability. Salesmanship perhaps, but not leadership ability.

Many would-be business leaders are specialists. They've established their ability with a collective enterprise. They often have graduate and even postgraduate credentials. They know their job and they know what's not their job. But frankly, if the toilet hasn't been fixed or the invoices haven't been sent out or a critical system is offline, they must be able (and willing) to become plumber, bookkeeper or IT manager all in one day. It helps therefore if the leader is practical, pragmatic and versatile. Or is accompanied by someone who is.

Ignorance

Believe it or not, some leaders simply don't know whether they are making money or not. Whisper this, because it's terrifying. Some leaders don't know how much they have at the bank and whether they can meet the payroll costs every month. There's no cash flow forecast, no overdraft facility negotiated just in case, there's no bank reconciliation. No one is taking responsibility. It is not the leader's job, but the leader must see that it is done. The leader must take responsibility.

It is quite common for businesses to go bust even with a full order book. If it cannot find cash to pay bills or wages, the company is dead. It may seem unjust, but business viability is just another basic qualification. This is summarized in the phrase 'cash is king'.

Lack of fight

Starting a company is not the achievement of the goal. It's the beginning. Anyone can establish a business. Anyone can run a business on a good day. But whether anyone can do this for three years is another matter. Many highly educated people get bored easily. They also lack grit to defend themselves against those who would do them harm.

There's no two ways around it, starting and growing a business requires aggression. It demands the ability to defend yourself and your colleagues from unscrupulousness. This can include those who would threaten you with legal proceedings for not paying for a substandard service. There are those who would deceive you about their ability and achievement at interview. There are those who commission work from you, knowing that they are about to go bust and leave you with the losses. There are competitors who would seek to blacken your reputation with lies. There are those who would seek to trick you with contract terms that are hidden or implied. There are those who would seek to impersonate you and your key players to embezzle money from outside the company. There are those who would launch a virus attack on your systems for no other reason than to cause you harm.

Invariably, these events choose their own timing. When they come together the leader can be dispirited, tired, ill, overworked and feel overwhelmed. But they have to somehow make it work. That they do is a miracle that few who have not done it can comprehend. This is why entrepreneurial leaders are so tightly bound. They have mutual respect based upon shared suffering. This creates a robustness, which can border on the blunt. It is not intended to be rude, but it often sounds that way and therefore can upset the sensibilities of liberally educated intellect.

It is the suffering and hardship that defines them. It is made all the worse because 'it is the smallest violin playing the saddest tune'. Nobody cares. So why do they do it? Well, ask them. For some, the financial rewards are a compensation. Some like the status and attention. Some are more phlegmatic. When asked, they have a look of the mountaineer about them. They do it because that's what they were born for. Because the challenge is there.

The suffering is what defines their success. They learn more from the suffering than they do from the success. That's why long-term entrepreneurial success is so deeply life changing. It changes their approach to leadership because it changes their approach to life. Henceforth, they become unable to accept that something cannot be changed or improved. Their learned skills combine to create that very rare type of person – someone who can change things.

Of course, these challenges are completely hidden on the day of start-up. No one likes to talk about the suffering, the defiance, the self-belief, the sacrifice, the lack of understanding, the difference in viewpoint. These are the ugly truths of entrepreneurship. It is distinctly un-middle class, but it helps if you can behave politely. It is certainly not academic, but it helps if you can assimilate techniques. It is unreasonable in every sense, although it helps if you can use reason. It will never allow you to be as fully complete as any specialist professional because you have to be commercial – that's a different mountain top.

No one likes to talk about the suffering, the defiance, the self-belief, the sacrifice, the lack of understanding, the difference in viewpoint. These are the ugly truths of entrepreneurship.

It helps if you are practical. It helps if you can wire a plug, change a fuse, iron a shirt, bake a cake, unblock a drain, nurse a child, start a reluctant car, paint a wall, fix a lock, build furniture, put up a sign, use a mop, clean a toilet and empty a bin. All of these tasks require prioritization, energy and action.

It helps if you can learn from other people how to interview, how to rebuild a server, read a balance sheet, reconcile a bank account, negotiate a contract and understand contract law, labour law, how to write marketing materials and make a presentation. And that's before you get to your own professional specialism.

Knowing when to defer to greater domain expertise is a matter of acquired judgement. Good leaders know there is little point 'having a dog and barking yourself'. Deferring to judgement is not the same as accepting an outcome. A good leader can be persistent with another's domain expertise. Where there's a will, there's a way. It is all a question of establishing a *joint* will.

Many commentators like to analyse entrepreneurship in an academic laboratory under controlled conditions, surrounded by referees and arbiters. In reality, entrepreneurship is a bloody mess, sanitized by media, heralded by retrospective financial analysis and condemned roundly by the ignorant as greedy, self-interested and ego-driven.

Ego

Let's face it, one of the reasons people want to be leaders is to feel important. They believe leadership is about telling people what to do. They enjoy the status of a limousine or business-class travel. This is a much worse problem among men because of overconfidence, as we have seen. But ego is just another type of personality defect. It places the needs of the leader above those of the team. It creates a different set of priorities. It places the leader's needs above those of the customer or the colleague. This is emotionally and economically inefficient.

Attitude and willpower matter because qualifications and knowledge do not necessarily bestow understanding.

For leaders in a post-industrial, tertiary age, the implications of this are far-reaching. The requirement for capital in business start-ups is minimal. The requirement for capital in all business change is minimal. In terms of leadership, the barriers to change have become minimal, so what is it that prevents leaders from changing?

A management cliché is that authority is never given, it's only taken. Most leaders have a lot more scope for change than they think. A positive leadership attitude can be transformational in terms of releasing the potential of colleagues. But this requires the leader to be motivated and interested in change.

The rising number of graduates and graduate thinking from business schools has created a perception that skills, training and knowledge are more important than attitude. They are not. The struggle for, and achievement of, qualifications creates an expectation that this really ought to be enough. But it isn't. Attitude and willpower matter because qualifications and knowledge do not necessarily bestow understanding. Remember, we're seeking to add balance, not just to be efficient in one direction or another.

A lack of empathy

Let's be clear about this. A leader can study a subject. They can get a degree in it. They can teach it. They can read every book on it. They can get a PhD in it. But they still might not understand it if the subject relates to human feeling. You cannot learn what pain, or hunger, or loneliness, or ambition, or joy, or disappointment, or misery, or despair, or hope, or hatred, or envy, or lust is like without experiencing it.

And this is the problem at the heart of leadership education. How do you prepare for leadership with just an academic mindset? You can't. Even worse, how can you train people for leadership who have never felt leadership?

Real leadership, especially entrepreneurial leadership, is deceptive. It looks like a leadership role, it uses many of the same techniques, but the sensation is night and day different. The experience of entrepreneurial leadership is *vivid*. It is haptic in the extreme. Everything feels more exaggerated and dramatic. The victories are inspiring. The losses are catastrophic. The relationships are stronger in every respect. The enemies are evil. The friends are more heroic. The range and proximity of polar opposite emotions can be terrifying to witness, for those of a more even academic disposition. This is why it's so counter to the liberal education culture. This may be more 'catholic' in its view, seeing both sides of the argument, but while this may be useful in negotiation, this sort of equivocation is death to entrepreneurial leadership.

The entrepreneurial mindset is that this is a life and death struggle. It's a battle for a vision to be seen and come to pass. It's not just a matter of profit, it's personal vindication, validation and vivification. This is why it's so misunderstood.

What doesn't cause business to fail?

There are many armchair diagnoses for business failure. These are the common ones, which are usually identified but which mask leadership failure.

Timing

It can easily be said that someone was too early or too late with a product, but that is to discount leadership's ability to recognize a position and change to it. A good leader will create a model that allows them to persist. There is no such thing as being too early for an opportunity, for instance launching in a recession. Either the world is coming to an end, in which case it doesn't matter, or things will pick up.

Lack of resource

'If only we had more money' is perhaps one of the most common causes of business failure. Investor money is, in reality, one of the most addictive substances known to mankind. Once a start-up becomes dependent, it is difficult to get off it. The entrepreneurial leader's first task is to minimize the expense required to make money, rather than concentrate on maximizing profit per se.

'Bad' people

Some of the best teams have been made up of substandard people. Why? Because there is no such thing. There is potential in everyone, especially young players who have much to learn and who appreciate guidance. Great leaders have transformational qualities. That's what makes them great. They seek out people they can help and forge bonds, irrespective of their provenance. There are many people from so-called 'bad' backgrounds, waiting for just that sort of leader who can recognize their potential. That's why leaders have to seek them out.

Competitors

By their very nature, start-ups face the challenge of incumbency. Leaders know that incumbency is a vulnerable position. Customers love to try something new, and so do employees. The challenger therefore must focus the proposition on what the competition is unwilling or unable to do. This is always the opportunity in incumbency.

Bad luck

Start-ups and their leaders will always face bad luck. It is better that they experience these things as soon as possible. Leadership needs the imagination to be able to see what might go wrong and lay contingency plans for it. Every good leader builds in resilience to be ready for the unexpected. This is also a matter of attitude. Some of the worst aspects of bad luck can be turned to great advantage. That is the thinking that all leaders must be aware of. The greater the setback, the greater the triumph.

Failure to win one big order

This is sometimes the trigger for failure, but in reality, business failure occurs before this. It does however create a convenient and viable narrative to explain the failure.

These are excuses for failure. They're not reasons for it. To find these we need to look at the leadership itself and to see how far from the zero model it has placed itself. Once we can find the imbalance (or multiple imbalances) then we're closer to the reason.

What makes a business start?

The law of entrepreneurship, and of business in general, is that there is always room at the top. The product doesn't have to be world-beating as long as it is better in some way. This could be a better price, better service, better location, better future, better for the environment. What dictates whether any of this happens is leadership.

If we were trying to analyse the balance between leadership styles, we might juxtapose these as thinking versus execution intersecting with individual and team (Figure 6.2).

This expresses the relationship between those who have plans for something and those who actually make it happen. Of course, there are plenty of people who can make things happen, but not come up with a new idea that needs to happen. That's why this model could be represented as reflexive.

FIGURE 6.2 The dreamer vs doer model

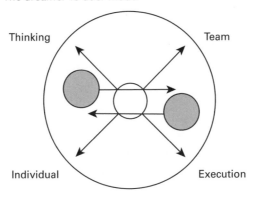

137

FIGURE 6.3 The bias to action model

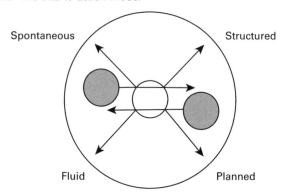

In a similar way, we can look at entrepreneurs and see what limits them. They frequently work between two axes of spontaneous versus planned intersecting with structured and fluid styles (Figure 6.3). For many entrepreneurs, their very spontaneity runs counter to any attempt to plan or structure their approach. It is why sole practioners remain so. Some entrepreneurs think structure causes decline. When you create job descriptions, you necessarily restrict potential in defining the territory the person is allowed to inhabit. Report lines and structures are necessary constraints. The larger the organization, the more bureaucratized and specialist it becomes and the less agile and cohesive.

Structure can also hinder flexibility and adaptability but is also necessary to grow. For this reason, many entrepreneurial businesses oscillate between the two quadrants above seeking a structure that is not incompatible with a 'bias to action'.

The model for success

In a similar way, we can assess entrepreneurial businesses using the intersecting axes of skills (Figure 6.4).

Here, we're looking at a key scale of entrepreneurial behaviour – whether they are essentially practical or not, and how

FIGURE 6.4 The entrepreneur model

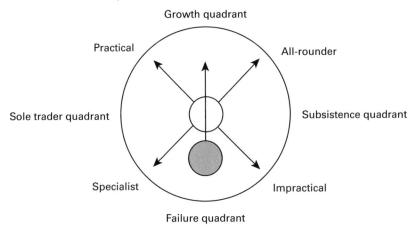

specialist they are. Those with all-round practical skills are more likely to grow because the early stages of start-up are ones where entrepreneurs need to demonstrate a multiplicity of skills, eg HR, IT, law, finance and logistics, in addition to their core business skills. This also explains why the entrepreneurial dreams of so many middle-class professionals come to nothing. It's just not enough to be a professional. You have to be a *commercial* professional. Sadly, the separation of these two happens at an early stage in academic education, where commercial courses have been much later additions to the ancient practices of teaching, law or medicine.

Ephemeralization

Back in the 1920s, the brilliant polymath Buckminster 'Bucky' Fuller began talking about the idea that we can make something out of nothing at all. He realized that technology keeps giving us the ability to do 'more and more with less and less until eventually you can do everything with nothing'.[23] This idea forms the foundation of Zeronomics – an economy in which the critical inputs are becoming ever more accessible and ever less expensive. He called this the 'ephemeralization' of the economy. Material and capital inputs are literally disappearing, vanishing before our eyes.

Bill Gates agrees. On this basis, he recommended a book, *Capitalism Without Capital* by Jonathan Haskel and Stian Westlake.[24] Gates explains that software is not like hardware: 'You don't need a lot of capital or overheads to produce software. You don't need a lot of capital.' He wrote, 'What is the best way to stimulate an economy in a world where capitalism happens without the capital? We need really smart thinkers and brilliant economists digging into all of these questions. *Capitalism Without Capital* is the first book I've seen that tackles them in depth, and I think it should be required reading for policymakers.'[25] MIT's Andrew McAfee echoed this idea in his book *More from Less*.[26] In it, he talks about the 'four horsemen of the optimist' – technological progress, capitalism, public awareness and responsive government.

This Zeronomics idea is not to be confused with ideas about recycling such as the circular economy. That term was introduced by the architect Walter Stahel in 1976 in a report he wrote with Geneviève Reday-Mulvey for the European Union Commission, called *The Potential for Substituting Manpower for Energy*.[27] The idea was simple. We should stop making and using single-purpose products that require us to dispose of finite materials so wastefully. Recycling should be inherent in this way of thinking. The idea was also to extend the useful life of products and to ensure multipurpose uses. In 1982 Stahel won a prize for his paper, 'Product-life factor'.[28] He argued that a longer and more varied product life diminishes the depletion of resources and reduces waste. There have been many ideas about how to reduce wastefulness and improve sustainability over the last century. Another is the cradle-to-grave (C2G) idea.[29] Here, the focus is on protecting the whole ecosystem from the harmful wastage of resources. Katja Hansen refined this notion even further by arguing that we could not only eliminate waste, we could eliminate the concept of waste.[30] She redefined waste as something that could feed future development. This harvesting and repurposing of waste is another way to create something out of nothing and harness more for less.

More recently, Jesse Ausbel of the Rockerfeller Foundation explained that what we are experiencing is the 'dematerialization' of the economy. Everything is becoming smaller and lighter, from silicon chips to tyres to dwellings.[31] Fewer and fewer raw materials are required. The number of hours required to make something is collapsing, even in manufacturing where laser sintering and 3D printing are allowing businesses to build more with less. Matter is dematerializing. This should allow new business leaders to create something out of nothing even more easily than before, which means we should think even more carefully about how to rebalance the flow of savings so that it waters more than a few rare hot house flowers.

Decapitalization of capitalism

Money is itself, as we shall see, dematerializing as we move from pieces of paper and coins to electronic and digital bits. What happens to capitalism when the capital inputs are not needed anymore? Can capitalism work without capital?

The internet and smart devices with apps now provide people with a means for building a business without needing any capital. Free online and smart device-based apps are platforms that permit businesses to scale. Apps create channels through which small businesses can get their products in front of many more people every day. In addition, people can now be paid for advice and recommendations. The 'influencer' community is essentially many individuals who exchange commentary for cash without needing to invest in building apps themselves. In other words, it is ever easier to create a cash-generating business with nothing but a smartphone. Capital is no longer an essential part of the process of building this kind of business. Capital is no longer as important as connections. Knowledge, networks, interactions with people and convening power carry ever more value in a world where the value of capital is falling.

Digitization of capital

We spoke earlier about Buckminster Fuller's view that the greatest resources in the economy would become more ubiquitous and cheaper every day – information and human knowledge, and now money. It is now clear that money, far from being scarce, is about to achieve a ubiquity never seen before. As we shift from paper money to electronic money, we may have missed the far more radical transition to digital money. In a world of digital money, policymakers can double or halve the money supply with a single keystroke. This explains why many governments, from China to the EU to Australia, have expressed an interest in developing sovereign cryptocurrencies.

Many have assumed that cryptocurrencies would be private forms of money like Bitcoin. It is assumed that crypto represents a means of escaping or leaving the realm of sovereign fiat money. But this isn't necessarily so. It is now possible to track virtually every single transaction in the economy due to the proliferation of Internet of Things devices and tracking systems that work through smartphones and chips embedded in objects, clothes, shoes, buildings and wearable devices. In theory, blockchain can become the means by which all transactions can be independently verified. For now, blockchain is still too slow to do this in real time. Policymakers like the idea, though. Chinese President Xi Jinping gave a speech at the 2019 Central Party Conference, in which he said the country should 'seize the opportunity' to deploy blockchain.[32]

Many took this to mean that the country would become more open and democratic. It soon became clear that China is interested in blockchain as a tracking device, not as a means of establishing a more open economy. The government passed a new 'Cryptography Law' in October 2019 that governs the use of passwords in preparation for sovereign crypto that will launch in 2020, which they call Central Bank Digital Currency (CBDC). If passwords are known, then transactions and movements are known. In a digital money world, governments believe that it will be nigh on impossible for a black economy to persist.

Of course, the balance between individual and state is a matter of geopolitics. What interests us though is whether this is a balanced approach.

Decapitation of capital

If capitalism is designed to ferret out profit opportunities, why doesn't the system naturally gravitate to those who are most efficient at finding the returns? Perhaps it is because we have been wrongly assuming that capital = capitalism.

The Queen of Hearts in Lewis Carroll's *Alice's Adventures in Wonderland* memorably said, 'Off with their heads' and 'Sentence first – verdict afterwards.' This captures the zeitgeist that has dominated public opinion about business leaders since the financial crisis. But, this kind of decapitation is neither wise nor advisable. However, there is another sort of decapitation under way. Business leaders have lost their heads in a multitude of ways – fraud, lies, cover-ups, as mentioned in Chapter 1. This is causing the public to question capitalism outright. But, what does capitalism look like without a leader heading it?

The answer may be in keeping with the zero theme. The best leaders are increasingly invisible. In the past, visibility and success went hand in hand. But today, in an era of deeper scrutiny and greater transparency, good leaders are finding they can accomplish more by being present less. Good leadership can be more easily measured by its absence than by its presence.

A good leader must go further ahead down the road, where they can see what's coming in the future. This means gravitating to the vanishing point. Guiding without feeling the need to be visible forces leaders to transfer more power to the team. When the team is empowered, the efforts acquire leverage. We've said that leadership is less about the leader these days and more about the ship. It is the leader's job to look ahead, over the horizon. The vanishing point has become an important destination that leaders should be aiming for.

This is not to say that the leader should be invisible. They just need to recognize that there are many more realities in which they need to be present, not just one.

To be clear, Zeronomics demands that our business leaders commit a kind of ego-suicide. The ascent into the vanishing point is an ascent into the light where the leader is ever less visible. It is where they provide illumination, where they become *fiat lux*. This is where Calvary substitutes for capital. This is where a leader becomes a presence and the guardian of a process, more than a person.

But you could not run an orchestra without a conductor! Actually, you can. The Grammy Award-winning Orpheus Orchestra in New York City[33] has not had a conductor since 1972. The New York Philharmonic performs *Candide* annually without a conductor in tribute to their former conductor Leonard Bernstein. You can run a train without a conductor, too.

In fact, almost everything you can think of is increasingly autonomous or capable of finding its way without a leader. That's the purpose of AI and machine learning. They expand our capacity for problem solving beyond the limits of our brains. Who will the leader be in that new world? Code? A computer? An algorithm? None of those things needs a leader. But humans do.

The lords of Silicon Valley have already anticipated this potential need for a new leader, a mathematical godhead. According to *Wired* magazine, the leading prophet of this new religion is a data engineer called Anthony Levandowski. The new religion of artificial intelligence is called Way of the Future (WOTF).[34] The documents state that WOTF's activities will focus on 'The realization, acceptance, and worship of a godhead based on Artificial Intelligence (AI) developed through computer hardware and software'.

That includes funding research to help create the divine AI itself. The religion will seek to build working relationships with AI industry leaders and create a membership through community outreach, initially targeting AI professionals and laypersons. The filings also say that the church 'plans to conduct workshops and educational programs throughout the San Francisco Bay Area beginning this year'.[35] It seems ironic that AI and machine learning will have leadership imposed upon them. It is no accident that the proposal is for a church of AI. Hardly anyone understands how AI, computers and algorithms really work. Those who do get paid very well.

For the rest of us, cybermancy (a simple faith in computers as oracles) is a new form of divination. This is the new universal religion whether we belong to WOTF or not.

Many effective organizations are virtually headless. Extinction Rebellion gathers millions of people together for climate change protests without anyone in particular being in charge. ISIS operates extremely effectively without specific or known leaders. Anonymous is a global movement with no discernible leader. In recent years, political parties have become energized by far greater public participation and yet by far fewer easily identifiable leaders. Who is the leader of the Democrats in America? It's hard to say. Is the President of the United States at the time of writing, Donald Trump, the leader of the Republicans? Not really. Many organizations and institutions are increasingly leaderless. The government of Belgium has not had a leader in place since 2011.[36]

If a leader is going to move towards the vanishing point, then they must know what the vanishing point is. It is an invisible space. The point at which imagination must take over from the facts because no facts are discernible over the vanishing point.

The purpose of a zero economy

What purpose does the economy serve? It is a means of allocating resources – capital, ideas, time, goods, services, rules, energy and materials that should all come together for the benefit of the citizens. A capitalist nation will define 'the good of the citizens' very differently than a dictatorship would. But, in all cases, the economy is a resource allocation mechanism. It's a sorting system that is guided by the relentless need to achieve ever greater efficiencies.

Technology today is making it ever easier to do more with less. Yet, people are spending ever more time at work. Is this driven by a fear impulse too? If I am not at work, surely I will fall behind. Is it driven by the desire to create an identity that can be more fully formed in the work environment than it can by life at home? Is it because our wants can never be fulfilled? The endless quest for more, bigger, best drives us into a slavish relationship with the economy. Or is it simply that we've forgotten or never appreciated that the economy was never supposed to take up all our time? If it is a system for allocating resources – time, capital, goods, services, human capital, intellectual capital – perhaps we are over-allocating human capital to the economy, and this is part of the leadership problem.

The point of work is to afford us the time and space to do things that don't pay but which give us joy, delight, fun, laughter, amusement and maybe even discipline and skill at things that don't pay. It is also true that we do our best work when our lives balance better between fun and rest and not just work and efficiency. Instead of using precious spare time to build personal brands and a degree of visibility, it might be more efficient to play. That's where we develop creative imagination and interact with the world in surprising new ways. It's not lost time. It's about stimulating the thought process more vigorously. Winston Churchill wrote a little book called *Painting as a Pastime* in which he explained that all brains need both rest and stimulation.[37] If you are reading for work, as a Cabinet Minister does, then reading for fun is no good. In his case, he began to paint, and he took up the hobby of bricklaying. This honed his skills of observation while resting his mind. This was an efficient thing for him to do given the demands on his time. That should prompt us to ask questions about efficiency.

Perhaps we have been defining efficiency too narrowly. Efficiency is useful but it isn't always better. We could create a robot to make a cup of tea, but the Japanese tea ceremony is an art form that has persisted through generations. It represents rituals, purity, harmony and respect for ingredients and time. Similarly, cooking food brings its own pleasures. Fast food is quicker and more efficient, but cooking gives us more opportunity to gather together and share stories and draw upon memories. It is in this deliberate down time that we find the head space to think more clearly, to shake the fear and to consider the role we play in choosing the leadership that we get. Charles Bukowski wrote a poem called 'No Leaders Please' that explains why leaders need to stop working.[38]

Perhaps we have been defining efficiency too narrowly. Efficiency is useful but it isn't always better.

In other words, being a leader requires fluidity and imagination. These are skills best learned through endeavours that typically don't pay financial rewards, but which offer rewards of imagination like sports, art, writing, dance, music, storytelling and even bricklaying. This is how our leaders can become more adept at the vanishing point. They start to paint and find out what the vanishing point really is. You can look at pictures of it. But it is only by drawing or painting that you begin to get a feel for the vanishing point.

Greater confidence and less fear about the future

Economies are continually changing. They don't just disappear. They're reimagined into something new. The jobs we may lose today are always replaced by some new sort of work tomorrow. The overwhelming fear of automation and robotics is grounded in the idea of scarcity. By reminding ourselves that the economy is actually driven by ubiquity, we might see the truth before us. The world economy today has record levels of automation and robotics, and also record employment. The two have gone together since the first robotic tool was introduced in 1804, which was the famous Jacquard weaving loom that the Luddites smashed to bits out of fear.

This will be accelerated by the COVID-19 pandemic and we can already see its effect, which is to accelerate trends that were there already. For instance, the drive to online and the leveraged use of videoconferencing to reduce cost and carbon footprint. For instance, the drive towards flexibility and agility. The lockdowns and subsequent releases have illustrated that businesses need to become more flexible. Long-term programmes have been projectized into exercises where a rapid acceleration has been followed by an equally rapid shutdown. This, of course, has profound implications for whole sectors, not just the 'gig' economy. The long-term effect of the pandemic may take a significant time to erase because the hit to confidence was so sudden and so prolonged after such a sustained period of expansion. This could be felt significantly in real estate (both commercial and residential), in entertainment and sports, in travel (especially business and luxury travel) and in events. The public sector with its increased job security may become a more attractive proposition. Some areas of the private sector may do well, especially those involved in food distribution, technology, healthcare, biotech and security.

Imagination

Zeronomics requires imagination. It's not that it's hard to imagine. It's that imagination is the essential magical power that allows a leader to transform from being visible to invisible. The vanishing point is not just a location on a picture. It is the leadership act of disappearing and only reappearing when the leadership is really required.

This idea of an invisible leader may leave some uneasy. What kinds of structures work without someone in charge? Buckminster Fuller gave a good deal of time to this question and concluded that one of the strongest structures was a geodesic dome. It is a circular structure, an architectural version of a circle, of a zero.

The original dome that he built in three weeks with his students back in 1948 still stands today at Bennington College in Vermont. What makes it so strong, especially for its weight? It is 'omnitriangulated'. The dome supports itself. It is not a bad analogy for the new generation of entrepreneurial leaders who are building their future using Zeronomics.

It may be that the highly visible allocators of capital have neither done the best job nor offer the best vision for allocating capital and resources in the future. Instead, the Zeronomics approach asks us to consider who is being most efficient with capital. It asks us to value inputs other than capital. The self-supporting nature is less about who has the most money and instead confers power on those who know how to convene and gather people together. The power to bestow confidence on entrepreneurial leaders may now be worth more and be better for society than the power to bestow capital. It may be hard to believe that we can build reliable and enduring economic structures in new ways.

Balancing is the key. The Zeronomic approach calls on us to balance better. No one wants a world where Apple, Uber, Beyond Meat or even WeWork cannot come to life. But we would like a world where more businesses get a shot at scaling.

Great businesses are undermined by their egotistical leaders all the time. We don't need fewer big business successes. We need fewer leaders destroying value for their own aggrandizement. Good stories often depend upon our willingness to temporarily suspend our disbelief. It requires love. The love of a better story is what opens the door for the stories of the real superheroes – those who, without advantage or even benefit, somehow create something out of nothing. That means we need more leaders who balance better.

Summary

Balance does not mean moving to only one side of the picture. We need to be more adept at placing ourselves anywhere within the landscape and making the best of what we find there. This too requires imagination, because courage comes from imaginary things. G K Chesterton put it beautifully when he wrote: 'Fairy tales are more than true – not because they tell us dragons exist, but because they tell us dragons can be beaten.'[39] The quality of our victories depends on the quality of our dragons. We have to create our own dragons.

Today the dragon is Adam Neumann at WeWork. Surely, we could create space for those who build better spaces and do it more carefully? You won't have heard of Ayesha Ofori. She is a former banker, who launched the Black Property Network and PropElle in the UK, which help black families and black women achieve financial independence through property investment. She says,

> I set my own agenda, I choose how to make my impact on the world and most importantly I get to be a present mum. I have a two-year-old daughter and being around for her is so important to me. When I'm immersed in the property world, I'm at my best. It doesn't feel like work. I read property news and articles for enjoyment and every time I'm outside I'm looking at buildings I pass to see if they have development potential.[40]

The dragon is not a person. It's the system that sees potential only in Adam Neumann and not in Ayesha Ofori. A Zeronomic society would give capital and confidence to both of these people but not blindly to the point of a catastrophe.

Is there any reason why businesses can't be established to be sustainable long term? An infinite approach does not demand that every business slows down and grows at a snail's pace. It just asks for more balance between many business models, many business leaders, many approaches to the building of value in the economy. It also asks whether business leadership, incentivized for the long term, would help curb the excesses, imbalance and egotistical behaviour. It's worth looking at this area in detail, which is where we go next.

CHAPTER SEVEN

Zero ego, zero gender

What role does the egocentricity of a leader play in the team? How does status change what the leader understands and has access to? How much does it obscure the vision and performance of the team? Why do leaders consistently overreach themselves? How can this be overcome?

To really understand a team, you have to watch it in action. For this reason, the Infinite Leader may want to be close to the team they're leading to be able to see the interactions. It's of paramount importance to understand the character of the team. Is it relaxed? Is it efficient? Is it dominated by one personality? You can hear it in the language they use. Are they focused on 'they', 'we' or 'I'? Do they appear to be having fun? If so, they're likely to get good at what they are doing. Character is as important in the team as it is in the leader. Character is destiny, so if you don't understand the character of the team, you won't know where it can go for good or for bad.

The leader's job is to know where the team is both physically and spiritually and to see the team in perspective. This requires a great deal of empathy with the team. This means the leader needs to know what it feels like to be in that role in the team. How do they feel they can make a contribution? What are they worried about? Can they see a future for themselves in the business? What will be their next career objective? This process is inhibited if the leader's ego requirements intervene. This is why egotistical leaders are seldom successful because they're not putting the team ahead of their own needs.

The notion of situational fluency is bound up with the leader's perspective. This is multifaceted. It involves understanding as much as possible about the people in the room. This requires empathy and the ability to see another's point of view.

In the game of snooker, players are always required to have one foot on the ground. It's the same with the leader. They need to maintain their grasp of the 'here and now' as well as the perspective or situational fluency. This is a demanding task and does not allow time for the leader to be focused on themselves. Every bit of their skill and concentration must be directed outside.

The gender model

This model uses the same principle, but is different again by virtue of the polarities. We can, though, assess leadership style in this model. Typically, we tend to see a leadership model that is too dominated by the individual and short-term, quantifiable goals as explained in Chapter 5. Usually this needs to be balanced with pressure from the opposite quadrant of the more long-term and collaborative.

This model is typically discriminative and wasteful of resource. We know for instance from the work of Chamorro-Premuzic[1] and others that masculine leaders tend to be focused more on personal goals and less on team goals. If we apply this thinking

FIGURE 7.1 The gender-equality model

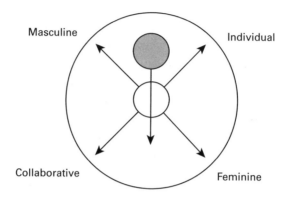

to the zero model, then it might show that gender imbalance is also a contributory factor to the leadership failure we've seen (see Figure 7.1).

The leader as actor

Again, to be able to fully represent the team, it helps if the leader is able to understand what each individual in the team needs. One of the qualities of President Trump's supporter base is they believe Washington is 'a swamp' that needs to be 'drained' and that the way it works is opaque. Trump understands this and invests a great deal of time in providing a running commentary through Twitter. This makes sure that the machinery of the state cannot filter what he's saying. Suddenly, his base is able to see and hear what he's doing immediately and without interpretation from the media. This reached an apogee in January 2020 during the impeachment hearings, when he tweeted 123 times in a day or pretty much every 10 minutes.[2] He acted as the commentator on the proceedings, so the voice he acted was that of someone constantly providing the countervailing opinion. He also recognized that it was a battle that he was likely to win and played up the threat that it posed, in order to make the victory look greater still.

Another quality of the Trump base is the anger that they feel about the waste of money in Washington. This is replicated in the tone of anger in his tweets, often using capital letters to emphasize a point. One of the reasons he has been enduringly popular with his supporters is that he's never changed the tone of voice and never stopped using his time to campaign. There has never been a US president who has used social media to such great effect.[3] As far as his base is concerned, he's appeared to display all the qualities of the leader they wanted him to be – communicative, garrulous, clear and consistent.

One of the things that great leaders become good at is reading the mood and deciding what approach to take or to tap into.

One of the things that great leaders become good at is reading the mood and deciding what approach to take or to tap into (or at least not be wholly out of kilter with). Whether you admire President Trump or not, there's no doubt he has applied this thinking well.

The difference between power and authority

All leaders know that they have power. The trappings of status are all around them. It's one of the things that often attracts them into the job. But do they stop for a moment to think about what these trappings of status indicate? Maybe they mean 'I'm not like you, so you can't have the sorts of conversations with me that you'd normally have with a colleague' or 'this shows that I'm much more important and that your status is lower'.

Certainly, power is easy to spot; what is less clear is the provenance of the authority behind the leader. Power is always separated from authority, for instance in government. Prime ministers and presidents have the power, but the authority resides with the people and the ballot box. In a similar way, in the modern corporation, the power is with the senior executives, but the real authority resides with the shareholder and ultimately with the customer.

Every leader looks powerful until you look further and see that behind every powerful figure is a different and separate authority. This could be shareholders, investors or the team itself. For instance, a manager at a football club may have power but the real authority is transferred from the supporters via the results that the team achieve. In a hospital, the doctor's authority may stem from their controlling professional organization or indeed from patient outcomes.

Leaders need to treat power and authority differently. The former needs to be familiar. The more frequently (and gently) power is exercised, the more it becomes embedded and therefore seldom challenged. This is like good policing. If an area has a culture of respect for the law, then seldom does it need to be enforced. The more familiarity there is with power, the less it needs to be used.

Authority though is different. This is much more mysterious. Think of the royal family. Very seldom is their power questioned because it is exercised gently and frequently. The authority of the crown, however, is much more mysterious. Where does the mystery come from? It can come from history. It can come from service. It can come from continued success. Authority, though, has different symbols of power. The latter has ephemeral status symbols, the former has enduring symbols. Institutions signal authority with a chain, baton, staff, rod or mace. There is considerable imagery surrounding the symbolism of authority. The US Congress has Roman symbols adorning the wall either side of the speaker's chair. Courtrooms usually seat the judge higher than the rest of the court. Height is always associated with authority. This is why courtiers bow. This is also why the immediate office of a monarch is called a court. The purpose of monarchy was to stand in judgement. The staff was often used to resolve disputes, as the monarch's staff was the one true measure, hence the term 'ruler'. This also accounts for the secrecy around Freemasonry. This was very much about stonemasons in its inception and about standards and measurements.

The problem with modern ego-based leadership is that all too often, it becomes quantitative not qualitative. It becomes about size and headcount rather than quality of thinking. This is the imbalance that leads to the short term over the long term, and individual rather than group goals.

The leader as judge

Very seldom in leadership books does anyone talk about the leader's role as judge. It's an important one, however. On board ship, for instance, the captain has the role of judge and cleric in addition to their operational leadership. Captains are vested with the authority to marry people or to convict them. A judge is neither prosecution nor defence. They are separate. The judge has to reflect the values of the courtroom – fair, unbiased, considerate of all evidence and information. For authority to be accepted, power must be dispensed fairly.

Leaders should develop the habit of speaking last in meetings.

For this reason, leaders should develop the habit of speaking last in meetings. First, this creates the perception that the leader is listening. Second, the ideas discussed may already be what the leader wanted to happen in any case. This allows the leader to try out an idea but to withdraw from it later if the idea doesn't work. Finally, the reason that leaders should speak last is because it is not their job to come up with the solutions (as much as they may like to boost their own ego), it's to make sure the team does. That way, there's more chance of the team accepting an idea – simply because they feel they created it.

This is also why the symbol of a courtroom is a balance scale. This is also used in assessing or assaying silver and gold for purity. Atop the Old Bailey, the central criminal court in London, is a blindfolded woman with scales in one hand and a sword in the other. This represents justice and authority equally balanced.

The dangers of over-deployment

The leader can't be focused on their team if they're 100 per cent occupied themselves. They must have spare capacity to be able to retain sight of the goal and other aspects of situational fluency. This means that the leader needs to be in an almost constant state of fluidity, empathizing with other participants in the team. Take a critical meeting, for example. The leader is not only aware of the objectives but is also capable of considering the viewpoints of other participants and thus has the ability to guide the collective outcome. Of course, the leader needs to be aware of his or her own role but is, in effect, keeping one foot on the ground at all times.

This is also why effective leadership needs to be physically fit. It will have to lend its energy to other members of the team to help achieve the goal. This can't happen if the leader is either short of energy or begrudges giving it to another team member. This is why physical fitness among leaders is so highly prized within military leadership.

This physical or kinetic intelligence is also a factor in being able to read the room. How does a person signal confidence in the way they move and talk? This tends to reveal itself in the person's posture and tone of voice. How does a person signal that they are listening and approachable? This could be shown in their face, where the eyebrows are raised, signalling that the person is actively listening and is engaged. What body language looks aggressive? This could be overly fixed eye contact, a narrowing of the eyes or moving physically closer to someone. How can you read whether someone is lacking belief? This can be seen in hesitation and a lack of eye contact.

To read all of these aspects of a meeting, the leader needs to be fully confident in their own role to the extent that they can spend time concentrating on others. Excellent leaders also recognize that individuals are far less nervous when focusing on the task in hand or on other people's issues, rather than their own.

The younger leader's greatest mistake is believing that they have to do more. They then don't have the time or the spare capacity to focus on the needs of those around them or to be able to handle unexpected crises.

The problems with status

Leaders have power and are often perceived as having more than they themselves actually recognize. The net result of this is the gradual exclusion of the leader from routine conversations and information flows. No one wants to tell anyone in authority if something goes wrong, so consequently the leader is bypassed. Conversely, when something has gone well, there's usually a flood of people trying to get to the leader first.

This illustrates how the leader's view of the world can rapidly become distorted. Either they do not see a problem until it's too late or they have an over-developed sense of how well the team is doing.

This progressive isolation can be countered only by leaders actively going beyond their normal report lines and talking to people. They must read and interpret what people are saying and how they are saying it. For instance, a leader can tell a great deal about the performance of a team by the tidiness of their workplace, especially in a factory where safety and tidiness go together.[4]

Isolation also promotes insecurity, which itself promotes insecurity in direct reports. The only way to alleviate insecurity is with more validation and ever more self-centred thinking.

To this end, the leader needs to be fully aware of the effect that their presence can have. Just walking around and talking to the team can sometimes be enough. The leader also needs to be aware of the effect their presence will have on a meeting. What is the purpose of the session? Will it be helped by the leader's presence? If not, then the leader should stay away. Leaders need to know what their own brand of values is, so it can be effectively deployed. Not every situation needs the leader's presence.

The choreography of leadership

We've forgotten how to use physicality. The Enlightenment focused on the mind. But, during this time, some important philosophers also emerged to speak about the relationship between mind and body.

Marsilio Ficino was an Italian scholar, Catholic priest and one of the most influential humanist philosophers of the Italian Renaissance. He was the first translator of Plato's complete extant works into Latin. His three books on life, published in 1489, provide a great deal of medical and astrological advice for maintaining health and vigour. He pointed out something similar to St Augustine, in that self-discipline is important in leadership. This is as much about controlling oneself as it is about controlling the perceptions of outcomes.

Ficino's notion of the angelic mind is where you find the Infinite Leader with one foot partly in the present but the other in a different, situationally fluent dimension. This is where it takes real skill to listen and also to be heard.

How does this apply practically? Let's take the example of 'working the room' – a key leadership skill. The leader knows the room is important, but he also knows that it takes physical and mental discipline to do it well. It requires quick-fire ways of both joining conversations and leaving them. It also means being able to recognize when a conversation should be joined.

Again, spotting a leader in a room is tricky and requires detailed acuity. In some Silicon Valley meetings, the leaders are the tallest, the loudest or even the ones with the best sneakers.[5] This deliberately creates a new set of rules, which makes it harder for instance for women to engage. Walking up and initiating a conversation is something that many find challenging for all sorts of reasons.

Being approachable in this context is also another skill. How does someone look approachable? It helps if you are on your own, but again this can be an uncomfortable experience for some. Wearing something different can help as a conversation starter. Some advertising people used to wear bow ties in order to signal that they were approachable and slightly out of the ordinary. It became a cliché.

Choreography is important here, especially when working with an international audience. This can be much more physical, depending on the country, signalling empathy with touch. Obviously, this requires care but it's useful to bear in mind that the Enlightenment focused on the mind of leadership. This is, again, why military leadership is different and often involves a high level of physical contact.

Shaking hands used to be the first sign of physical leadership. You can immediately tell a great deal from the first handshake. Sometimes this is backed up by either a two-handed shake or a slap on the back, especially among men. If the handshake is weak, this can be interpreted as unreliable. Some men have a technique of grabbing the hand then rotating their hand through 90 degrees so that their hand is on top. This is known as getting the upper hand. It is thought that the phrase came from US playgrounds. To determine who gets first choice of player when picking teams in baseball, one team captain grabs the bat at the bottom, the other captain takes hold above the first's hand. They then progress hand over hand until they reach the top. Whoever is left holding the bat gets the 'upper hand' and has first choice.

Power needs the continuity and clarity vested in two-way communication. Authority doesn't need any two-way interaction. It is a broadcast phenomenon. Power does. Authority *is*.

Perhaps the greatest problem with the egotistical leader is that they are insecure and this tends to attract others with similar deficiencies.[6] This is the basis for one of the most dangerous and toxic leadership situations. That of an arrogant leader with a submissive team. This is why diversity is so important in the team make-up.

Symbols of leadership

We're all familiar with the status symbols that leaders have. These include the executive car or driver, first- or business-class lounges and travel, the large empty office, the expense account, the personal staff, the chair at the top of the table. These are all quite common in the office environment, but the wise leader will be aware that all of these items come with a side effect. They reduce communication with the world as experienced by everyone else. They do this by making leaders physically harder to get to.

All of this inhibits communication. This is like being a judge who is so deaf they cannot hear the cases for and against. This means they don't hear the minority voices. And this is where danger lurks. All new ideas arrive first as a minority voice. Early adopters are the minority of a potential new market. For this reason, leaders need to guard against 'the tyranny of the majority'. This was an idea first developed by philosopher John Stuart Mill. He pointed out that the majority view needs to be continually challenged to validate that it is still current.

In this respect, when the leader performs as a judge, they assess on one hand the future, and on the other, the incumbency or status quo. The leader then sits at the point where the future meets the past in terms of thinking. If they shift their balance forward, then the future arrives. If they shift backwards, the past or present dominates.

Closely linked to this is the amount of dissent that leadership hears. Well, no one in their right mind is going to tell the boss that they are stupid. But if the boss asks for an opinion about something, they grant permission for feedback. This is also so much easier when the leader gets away from all of the symbols of power.

The future and new ideas and new people are types of dissent. The leader signals their willingness to change by how much and how willingly they embrace change and new ideas. To do this, they must be prepared to experiment and establish the principle of ideas that are STT, or 'safe to try'. If the consequences of trying a new idea or a new approach or process are negligible, then why not try it?

'What do you think?' These are the four most powerful words in the leader's vernacular.

There are many senior executives who will play retail customer or go and talk to different people to pick up ideas for improvements. This is useful when done anonymously, but it's also highly motivational when someone senior asks 'What do you think?' These are the four most powerful words in the leader's vernacular.

The leader as custodian of assets

The notion of balance finds its way into the long-term custodianship of assets. These are more than just what is accounted for. This is one of the gross peculiarities of wealth creation. Most of what constitutes an asset for the business is not actually recorded. Take the chair that you are sitting on. An organization somewhere knows its value. It can tell you what it paid for it, it could tell you the resale value, it could probably even tell you what it would cost to replace it. But it couldn't tell you anything about the value of the ideas that we're generating together while you are sitting in it. This is the great curiosity of accounting in that most of what really constitutes value is termed as 'goodwill'. It sits on the balance sheet as a deductible item imputed by the value of the assets.

This is why the leader needs to consider the balance between the new and the status quo, and the balance between the tangible and the intangible.

What is a responsible person? They normally speak in a reasonable tone, they have a standard of behaviour. Above all, they demonstrate *judgement*. One of the tests of whether someone can be considered as a director of a limited company is whether they are a 'fit and proper person'. What does this mean? The British government says: 'There is no definition in the legislation of a "fit and proper person".' That's not very helpful is it? It basically omits those who have been disqualified as directors or involved in tax fraud or other fraudulent behaviour including misrepresentation and/or identity theft.

So, leaders have a fiduciary duty to behave in a 'fitting' manner. It is this curious lack of acuity that catches many leaders out. They see the authority and the objective and some may even see the task to be carried out, but most do not see the implied obligation to behave in a responsible way. If they are determined not to do good, then they should at least not actively do bad.

It's a moot point but worth asking any leader: What are the values of your organization and team and in what way do you live those?

Leaders and the future

The leader is primarily a custodian of values. This is why good leadership spends time not just predicting one outcome but preparing plans for many outcomes. This notion of confidence underpins so many aspects of leadership in so many walks of life. It's certainly vital in business, but it's also important in justice, education, healthcare, the clergy, transport (eg the pilot of an aircraft), the architect, the engineer, etc.

Too few leaders remember that so much of their narrative needs to be about preparing for a future. This means the ability to look at shared outcomes, ie what will always be required, under any circumstances, in the future?

Well, people that are positive, practical, hard-working and good humoured. For this reason, no matter what the economic cycle, leaders are always looking for these qualities.

This is another reason why older leaders have difficulty laying out a future, for instance if they are in their 70s or 80s. For obvious reasons, the leader may not be trusted with a long-term plan because they might not be around to see it.

Leaders are key to confidence in the future. Leaders make other people feel confident. All futures are dominated by faith, indeed capitalism doesn't work without faith in the future. If there isn't a sense of deferred gratification, then why would the saver save or the student study to pass exams or to learn a skill? Capitalism works because people believe it works. Confidence is faith. So, it could be said that stock markets have something in common with organized religion. They both rely on and are driven by faith.

In many instances, this faith is reflected as confidence. This is what drives markets and is often also one of the key determinants in whether leadership is seen as successful. The leader isn't there to demonstrate competence in the present. The leader is the custodian of the future.

What is charisma?

Charisma in leadership is hard to objectively pin down. What appeals to one person might repel another. But during the

funding rounds for WeWork some journalists noticed the tall-
ness of Adam Neumann and some even commented that he had
'a mane' of hair.[7] Elon Musk is over six feet tall. Jack Ma is 5′2″.
The point here is that charisma is never average and sometimes
it can be self-perpetuating. Someone appears charismatic because
everyone says they are.

Physically unusual traits might lead to an air of mystery about
a leader and this is linked to the concept of value. All value is
mysterious. Take for instance the price of Damien Hirst's jewel-
encrusted skull entitled 'For the Love of God'. It sold in 2007 for
$100 million. No one can say why. It just did. It sold for what
someone was prepared to pay for it. Impenetrable mystery is at
the heart of value. It can look almost indistinguishable from
madness. Indeed, both lack logic. But one is legitimized by
money. Logic doesn't work in this realm. That is why when
investors turn on a charismatic leader, it's a story everyone
recognizes – *The Emperor's New Clothes*.

This is ultimately one of the curious things about the super-
rich investor. They back leaders for reasons other than logic. At
that level, what matters more to the investor, making money or
having such a bizarre perception of value that it moves markets
independently? They display the ultimate in confidence in an
item of questionable value and thus, it becomes a self-fulfilling
prophesy. This is why money tends to make money.

Leadership 'light'

Leaders have convening power. Wherever they go, they attract
attention. This can be useful when it comes to sharing attention,
especially in areas that normally don't receive any. The leader's
job is thus not to illuminate everything but to illuminate some
things with great clarity. It is to provide chiaroscuro – the light
and the shade of how and what the team sees around them.

The leader as shaman

Tribal shamen are not the most experienced or the most skilled. They are the most trusted. They are the people to whom the tribe turn when faced with a crisis. These are not always official positions, but social ones. Quite frequently, for instance, this might be a receptionist rather than someone in HR. They don't tend to seek the limelight. For this reason, leaders always do well to stay close to ambassadors of this sort.

How technical change is undermining personal authority

How does technical change affect authority? It changes the balance of power. It is shifting the power towards those who appear to control the technology. Remember *Jurassic Park*? The leader was not the professor with the most knowledge and experience. The most powerful person was the programmer controlling the fences that kept the dinosaurs in.

Perhaps the most powerful way in which technology changes power is with what it remembers. Take for instance litigation or personal law. There might be a statute of limitations for litigation to be disclosed of say five years. Google, however, might link any search for a person or company to that litigation for much longer than five years. The facts may therefore not be disclosable, but they certainly are discoverable. The more information is gathered, the more history and track record are ever present. Who controls data, controls memory and decides what can be forgotten? This is especially important when it comes to reputation or brand because whoever controls the data becomes the custodian of the past. You can see this emerging already on any review site, eg Tripadvisor. If you don't control the data, you can't control ultimately how history records facts.

Summary

Most leaders exist at the centre of their own universe. Leaders with this attitude will insist on being the centre of other people's universe as well. For some, this will be true. So, the leader must recognize that the values of their community are projected onto them. This is a tremendous responsibility, but it's also a great privilege if you consider it to be so. You have the power to make people feel good or bad according to your role. Not many people get the opportunity to make a difference in other people's lives, but leaders do. So, why do so many do it so badly? The answer is ego. The power and the status make them feel important. Well, they do temporarily. The problem with this type of ego-based leader is that the desire for self-validation will keep resurfacing. This sort of need can never be fulfilled.

It is OK to create the centre of things, but you don't need to *be it*. If that's the case, then the culture will not be sustainable. The thing that should be at the centre is the culture. This, ultimately, is what will endure, way past the leader's involvement.

If you have to be at the centre, then think of it more like a solar system in that the sun holds everything together and provides the warmth and daily rhythm for the success. This is an infinite process because it's not just the balance of the leader we seek. A good leader will subordinate their own needs to the task of balancing the team and the community.

We fall into the problems of egotism partly because of the way we are educated. We're encouraged to be individualistic, competitive and win at all costs. That's why education is also worth exploring in the next chapter.

CHAPTER EIGHT

Zero education

How do we prepare leaders for their futures? What changes are needed in their education? Who should they learn from? What are the barriers to changing this? Is there a role for spirituality in defeating unethical behaviour? What are the inherent shortcomings of the education system as it prepares us for the future?

In the first instance, there has to be an admission that the way we're preparing leaders is contributing to their lack of balance. We have too much emphasis on the Western reductionist principle of analysis and data, and not enough on reading the mood and interpreting feelings. Facts are simply not enough anymore. It's no good the major corporation saying that it pays all of its taxes legally, if the total proportion of tax paid is minor. The feeling this creates matters. We may be able to point out that something is legal, but that does not make it moral. The fact that a corporation is guilty of polluting a river and has paid a fine in no way erases the damage to trust.

Good leadership should have a nurturing aspect that raises an organization's culture and an employee's values to higher levels of ethical behaviour. By demonstrating ethical leadership, a higher level of integrity is possible. This promotes greater trustworthiness and encourages the team to accept and assimilate the vision and values of the group.

Good leadership should have a nurturing aspect that raises an organization's culture and an employee's values to higher levels of ethical behaviour.

An important part of how we look at leadership is the context that's given to it by our education. This colours our whole perception of what it means to be a leader. So, for instance, is it about leadership as a single person or is it about an attitude that can be shared by everyone? Teams are far more effective if it's the latter. Schools and universities, though, are a competition between individuals. They are designed to produce a winner and a loser when everyone is grouped by the same year of birth. But in what walk of life do people come together grouped by their year of manufacture? Perhaps the military, but that's it. Our education systems are designed for someone – an individual – to win a prize. The problem is that outside the education system, out in the real world, it's not as simple.

The leader's job is to ensure that the contribution of each individual is maximized. This means maximizing the qualities of collaboration, empathy, patience, consistency, loyalty and integrity. These are all qualities that are not emphasized or assessed in education. You don't get a better class of degree by assisting your cohort to get theirs. The education system is geared to make individual attainment synonymous with leadership. It isn't. This assumes that the objective of every team is for one individual to 'win'.

The answer to the question then, 'what makes a good leader?' (and by association, 'what qualities do they need to have?'), is that 'it depends' on what the objective of the group is. So what might alternative team criteria be?

A leader might be there for 'survive and thrive' criteria. This might be defined as family leadership. We're not trying to hit a specific objective, but we're still providing leadership, support and protection, nonetheless.

Similarly, for a leader in a 'least-worst outcome' organization, for example in a hospice dealing with end of life care, the criterion might be to provide a dignified death. Again, there's no quantified objective although there may be many significantly subjective criteria. In this case, the leader needs sensitivity, patience and compassion.

Let's take military leadership for instance. The objective cannot be just to beat the enemy because no one knows if there will even be an enemy. The objective then is to have the team fully trained and prepared for all outcomes. It's still leadership but not necessarily with an immediate objective that can be 'won'. Military leadership must also constantly reinforce the commitment to the country, the national interest, the cohesion of the unit, even if the military is not called upon to act.

Marks and grades

Education has come to be dominated by scores, marks and grades. The pressure starts early and it goes all the way through to GPA (grade point averages) and GMAT[1] scores. They are very important because they dictate life outcomes. Students sometimes kill themselves because of them.[2]

How did it come to this? During the industrial revolution, students were plentiful and teachers were rare. In 1792, William Farish, a tutor at Cambridge University, came up with a method that would allow him to process more students in a shorter period of time. He invented a grading system that had originated earlier in factories as a way of determining if shoes made on the

Education has come to be dominated by scores, marks and grades.

assembly line were 'up to grade.' It was used as a benchmark to determine if workers should be paid and if the shoes could be sold. This grading method standardized assessments, increased throughput and reduced the hours in the classroom.

In other words, the school system was established like a factory with standardization, quality control and production targets both at the input and output level. This would be fine if everything we subsequently go on to do is process and production line orientated. Of course, there are standardized processes, but we're not leading processes and machinery, we're leading people. So, why have we never reformed the systems? There has been change but education has become highly politicized, concerned less with what is efficient and more with what promotes social mobility. Furthermore, the vast majority of education is carried out in the state sector with top-down, centralized controls. The revolution in free schools like the Leigh Academies in Kent, for instance, has addressed the gap between those students destined for academic achievement and those for other walks of life.[3]

After Farish had completed his system, he no longer needed to look at individuals to know if they understood a topic, his grading system would do it for him. The problem with this is that it's now possible to get a degree and still not understand the subject. For instance, you could study pain, read every book on it and correctly answer questions on the theory of it. If you'd never felt it though, could you say you *understood* pain?

Farish's system would assess with equal efficiency 20 or 200 children. He brought grades to the classroom and the transformation was both sudden and startling. Within a generation, the lecture hall/classroom had been industrialized. Students who scored high marks were good and those with low ones were bad. It was a system that was designed for academic processing efficiency and on the surface of it, more students were taught to an independently verifiable standard.

The side-effect of this is threefold – first, to make the process, together with the institution, rather than the people, the most important output. Second, it makes our leaders those who were trained to pass exams individually, rather than to lead groups of people. Finally, it teaches a uniformity of thought approved by third-party verification. Perhaps this explains the political involvement. Who controls education controls what is perceived as education.

Thus, graduates enter into the world of collective endeavour with next to no preparation. The result is a delayed progression to leadership, a dawning sense of disillusionment and the realization that so little preparation has been purchased at such great cost.

The price of education

Graduates today are therefore likely to have more debt – a major disincentive to those from poorer backgrounds. Worryingly, they're also more likely to think alike.

This is our fault. That's the view of Sir Anthony Seldon, historian, biographer and Vice-Chancellor of Buckingham University (BU).[4] What sets BU apart is that it's the UK's only not-for-profit private university. He makes the point that if you don't teach ethics and morality, pupils won't learn it:

> We have a situation where Gradgrind[5] is running most education systems around the world. Anybody who says you can reduce the purpose of education to the passing of tests is guilty of adopting that approach. Exams and tests matter but they're not all that matters and the problem is they are seen by many to be all-embracing.

We need leaders who can think independently and creatively, not just pass exams that have been verified independently by those whose main role is to perpetuate the system.

The following is an extract from Robert P George's concluding statement at Education 20/20. George is an American legal scholar, political philosopher who serves as the McCormick Professor of Jurisprudence and Director of the James Madison Program in American Ideals and Institutions at Princeton University. So, he's not exactly under-educated.

> You're sending those of us who teach at the college level increasingly diverse students... But I'm also seeing something else and it's not what we want or should want. Students who are diverse in myriad ways and yet alike in their viewpoints and perspectives and prejudices. Students who have absorbed what I call the *New York Times* view of the world. They think what they think they're supposed to think. They seem to have absorbed uncritically progressive ideology and they embrace it jealously, obediently and alas dogmatically, as a faith, as a kind of religion.[6]

This shows the futility of argument about whether a leader is 'good' or 'bad'. It's spectacularly unhelpful. Good for what? Bad at what? Academically qualified but without understanding? Not qualified but with great understanding? First, the criteria are subjective. Second, it depends solely on what the objective of the team is. Invariably, this is a balance between qualitative and quantitative objectives. Third, it depends on the perspective. A weak team member might rate the leader more highly if they tolerate weakness in the team. A strong member might disagree and believe it imposes more of a burden on the rest of the team.

Let's look at qualities which in education are sought after as markers for future leaders. In school, in university, at work, we get 'marks', we get scored (Table 8.1). Later in life we get scored with money and status.

The qualities on the right-hand side of the scorecard are the important leadership qualities, but only in so far as they fit the task and team at hand. They would not normally be measured at school or university. Why? Are they not just as important for

TABLE 8.1 Education scorecard

We get scores for:	We get nothing for:
Right answers	Empathy
Obedience	Non-conformity
Individual achievement	Collaboration
Passing exams	Teaching others
Action	Endurance
Attention	Imagination
Deduction	Determination
Maturity	Humour
Intellect	Humility
Organization	Integrity
Opportunism	Loyalty

leadership? The qualities on the right-hand side may be illegitimate for leadership selection.

If we accept that in actuality, schools and universities treat these skills as incidentals or *nice to haves* then it's why we're churning out leaders who continue not to 'get it'. The problem is therefore hiding in plain view. Earlier, we pointed out that the number one cause of CEO failure is 'ethical lapse'. Can we not draw a line connecting what we teach at the early levels of education with this specific result in mind?

It's also difficult to assess integrity, determination and humility independently, but they are important, nonetheless. This, then, forces us into the realm of judgement.

It would appear that all the skills listed on the right in Table 8.1 are important to teams yet illegitimate for leadership selection. Worse, the skills on the right are also those most frequently (and often disparagingly) associated with 'feminine' traits (see the works by Tomas Chamorro-Premuzic referred to in Chapters 1 and 7).

Feeling as well as thinking

Perhaps the trend we can see among almost all leadership these days is that intellectual thinking has become more dominant. We have created leaders who believe that people commit only when they understand. No. They commit when they feel understood. That's different. Not everything that counts can be counted.

We need leaders who can listen and converse to seek understanding. Can you teach graduates to think in this way? The very logic of their processes might deny something as illogical as feelings. In the same way that love doesn't parse, education may not be teaching you to think properly. Many people analysing this statement won't 'get it'. They will analyse and critique without seeing the bigger picture that the analytical approach is part of the problem. The critique is all they know.

It might well be impossible to convince the educated that their greatest asset may also be their worst liability. Don't forget that many have spent 20 years in a system. This system is reflexive and self-congratulatory. Graduates go on to get postgraduate qualifications so they can teach students how to become graduates. Of course, the system couldn't be wrong, otherwise we'd be undermining what cost us (and our parents) dearly. It defines us. It defines our friends. Who we are. Where we live. University is one of the great rites of passage. It's really difficult to admit it may have its shortcomings. But there are ways.

Ideas may follow analysis, but the process does not necessarily create them. Think of the brain as being elastic. When pushed in one direction analytically, it recovers in the opposite direction. Analysis is followed by synthesis. Analysis is the 'left-brain'. Synthesis belongs to the 'right-brain'. How do we know this? Well, we have Einstein, who wasn't stupid, but his boss thought he was. He used to be a patent clerk.

Einstein's biographer, Walter Isaacson, shared Einstein's thoughts on solitude in his book *Einstein: His life and universe*:[7]

I am truly a 'lone traveller' and have never belonged to my country, my home, my friends, or even my immediate family, with my whole heart; in the face of all these ties, I have never lost a sense of distance and a need for solitude.

Einstein spent a lot of time away from his friends, family and work. He did nothing but think, often in complete isolation. He went for long walks, played his violin or went sailing. These moments of solitude were the provenance of Einstein's ideas.

Ironically, Einstein complained about the distractions of various devices his discoveries made possible. And he didn't have 24-hour news and social media to contend with.

Most graduates will shyly admit to this. That their really, really good ideas – the epiphanies – have a strange way of coming about. Everybody has them. Graduates or not. And how they happen is worth discussion. They are peculiar. Einstein knew that great ideas often reveal themselves in solitary moments. Most often when not at work. Most often when not trying. For some, even when they're asleep.[8] It seems we have an inbuilt capacity to join the dots. But we have to find the time to stop.[9] This is difficult for anyone to do. It is almost impossible for politicians.

The point here is worth labouring. Great thinking doesn't involve either analytical processes or conceptual processes, but both.

The spark

It's very difficult to define this. It's impossible to teach it. But some people just have a certain something about them. It's difficult to pin down, but you know it when you see it. What is it? It comes down to a variety of different skills, but what these add up to is flexibility. They look like they will be at ease under almost any circumstance imaginable. They seem to have the ability to move between the two columns of the education scorecard almost at will, and instantly. This is what we mean by balance. It's not just about being able to stay in a state of equilibrium but a resilience to the forces that cause destabilization. Balance is a habit, a state of mind.

Of course, at the core of this is energy. No leader can get away without it. But it's more than this. Most leaders have a passion for what they do. Almost as if it's the only really important thing that matters to them at present. For this reason, they have the capacity to make those around them feel special. Anyone can learn this. It's the concentration on the little stuff. Checking in regularly. Making sure that they are prepared. Bringing them up to speed on a discussion. Being alert to any problem they face. Most good managers have this skill.

Of course, this should work from the leader down. What's less obvious as a hallmark of leadership is that it should work upwards too. What really separates and elevates leaders is their ability to manage upwards. Of course, subordinates like having someone to update them, talk to them, help with their problems. But leaders like this as well!

The myth about leadership is that it works in one direction only. The point here is that it doesn't just work downwards and upwards, it works in every direction. It's quaquaversal, which stems from the Latin *quaqua versus* meaning 'turned wheresoever'. Leadership is leadership no matter whether it's going up the organization, down it or sideways out of it. The leader's job is to focus all their activity on other people irrespective of whether they can be of benefit. This then creates an example not just of intellect or skill set, but of ethics, too. When this happens, organization leaders then become community leaders.

Some might say: 'I'm a leader. I don't have time for this.' You always have time to do good. No matter how small or how large, leaders always make the time. The fact that they are busy but have found the time makes the gesture or intervention all the more powerful. Most leaders have no concept of the power they carry in their ability to reward or recognize. It doesn't take money. It doesn't take status. It takes a moment's consideration.

It is difficult to pin down what drives some people to take on this responsibility. It could be about expectations. It could be down to how much they feel the responsibility. What we can say though is that it's rare. Whenever we find it, we need to elevate it. The really great leaders though are modest about

You always have time to do good. No matter how small or how large, leaders always make the time.

elevating their profile for all the reasons already identified. They don't even know they're doing it. Maybe it's a higher calling?

The moral dimension

There are courses for church leaders where they can combine divinity studies with business administration. This allows them to run church administrations more effectively. But what we're talking about here is leaders who are aware of a higher spiritual calling than just the making of money or the gathering of power.

In many respects, if we compare commercial leadership from century to century, we can point to the fact that our world has become more technical, more global, more professional, more diverse, more efficient, more litigious, more interconnected. But it is difficult to point to how the behaviour of business has become more moral.

Maybe this doesn't matter? Why does business need to do good? Why does it need to be concerned with its reputation? Well, in the short term, you could argue that it makes no difference. But, as we've explained, more companies than ever before have had their reputations fall apart and their business destroyed as a result.

This is especially the case in banking and financial services. This is an industry that should have trust at its centre. But all that trust was completely destroyed in the great crisis of 2009. If you destroy trust in finance, which is supposed to be the most conservative of professions, then by association you devalue trust in all other areas.

The tyranny of the orthodox

The lack of morality has become an existential threat to leadership.

But is it enough to point out that if leaders do not behave they will destroy themselves? How have we come to the point where we even have to think before we point it out? Because we've come to accept some leadership principles as sacrosanct, for instance:

1 We have become overly focused on the short term. Five-year plans are now considered acts of fantasy. Most organizations are now managed quarter to quarter. The average tenure of CEOs is falling.[10] The average length of service of all employees is falling.

2 We have become overly focused on quantitative measures of success. Financial targets have come to dominate decision-making as an indicator of success. Of course, they are an important indicator, but there are others like customer satisfaction.

3 When thinking about leadership, we have become entranced by the leader and ignored the 'ship'. We've discussed how we've become focused on the halo leader as passed down to us by religious icons, eg Jesus or Moses. These leaders are male, middle-aged and mysteriously visionary.

4 Leadership has become too separated from the community and its goals. This is reflected in the increase in multiples that

the leader earns over the lowest-paid member of staff. It's also illustrated in what is expected of the leader – to be superhuman, the hardest working, the smartest, the most present. This makes it harder for diversity to embrace leadership because it appears to be something that only superhumans can do.

5 Government has stepped away from 'moral' leadership because of the decline in organized religion. No complaint with this, but religion is not the same as morality. Government has a role to play in setting standards of behaviour and probity. One of the best ways it can do this is by knowing when its presence is required and that government is not always good government.

6 We've stopped caring about 'local' issues. As leadership has become more focused on quantity, it has gone further in pursuit of it. This has driven it further from its local causes. This is reflected in the rise of the urban area as a location of economic and political influence. Now, cities and mayors are becoming more important than presidents and prime ministers and countries.

7 We have made our leaders focus on achievement rather than maintenance of values. For instance, now it is common for leaders of charitable and third-sector organizations to be known as a chief executive. This is a title copied from business leadership. How would we feel if our local church was no longer run by a vicar, father, pastor, imam, rabbi or Granthi but a chief executive?

8 We have devalued and dismissed those who care for and protect others, our nurses, our home-carers, our teachers and our police services and military. None of these careers offers substantial financial or fringe benefits and therefore they are not seen as fast-track careers. These people are as much, if not bigger, heroes as any entrepreneur or business leader.

9 We've become convinced that exterior sources of finance are always the best way to grow a business. Whatever happened to patient reinvestment? There's also a notion that without

professional financing a business is doomed to low growth and poor prospects. A company without a 'burn rate' is considered to lack imagination. In other words, the firm is expected to spend far more than it earns in preparation for a vastly larger customer base than it currently has. Even though this model rarely actually works. Maybe this explains why so few businesses make it to profitability and success. The problem isn't the business, it's the financing model and the belief system that underpins it.

10 Finally, we've become overly committed to the notion that only skills and education matter. We have virtually no discussion or education or training around attitude and the difference that attitude can make. There are no classes on it at any level in education and it's certainly not present in postgraduate training. Yet, its influence on successful outcomes is paramount. Within attitude we could place determination, resilience and a sense of humour. None of these things is formally assessed in examinations or in job interviews because they cannot be measured scientifically.

It's not just that formal education is flawed. It's that it's simply not enough.

How do we change the way education operates?

In short, we will have to change it gradually, perhaps so slowly that the existing system is simply bypassed instead. The free school movement has fundamentally changed the approach to secondary education. The same change is now overdue in leadership education.

First, leaders don't need to have a university degree. Of course, there are great advantages to education, but the chief reason for getting educated is to open up the person to new ways of thinking and to question what they have learned. According to the US Census Bureau,[11] 90 per cent of Americans have finished high school but roughly only one-third have a university degree.[12] That means we are typically excluding two-thirds of the population from leadership roles. It cannot be true that none of them has leadership potential.

Leaders don't need to have a university degree.

We also have to recognize that preparation for business management is not leadership training. Business management requires a strong grounding in a broad practical skill set. Leadership involves different skills, closer to those we have listed above.

The education system is about people. These people are split into two groups: students, and teachers and lecturers. The majority of teachers and lecturers are graduates, often from families who are graduates themselves. They work in a system that emphasizes:

- individual, rather than team-based, achievement;
- academic and analytical prowess;
- compliance, rather than rebellion and independent thought;
- short-term rather than long-term goals;
- that the worst consequence of cheating is expulsion and censure.

This academic environment is free of multiple pressures of time, finance and competition. In the outside world, there are significant rewards for cutting corners and it is often these, rather than incompetence, that generate unethical behaviour.

Leadership as a calling

Father Dwight Longenecker is the Pastor of Our Lady of the Rosary Church, in Greenville, South Carolina, in the US. Writing

FIGURE 8.1 The egocentric model

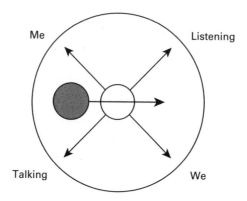

in *The Imaginative Conservative*,[13] he outlines Benedictine principles for business:

> According to the rules, they promise to pursue a life of stability, obedience and conversion of life. The root of the word obedience is the Latin for 'listen'. So, the vow of obedience becomes the demand to listen.

Successful leaders should begin by learning to listen. Remember the egocentric model? See Figure 8.1.

This means listening to the market, listening to suppliers, customers and staff.

Another Benedictine vow is for a life of stability:

> This means promising to remain faithful to one community for life. For the modern leader, the vow of stability points the way to a stable attitude towards the team. Stability in the business context means building strong and sure foundations, avoiding unnecessary risks and investing for the long term.

Longenecker adds:

> ... it is through leadership and the application of ethical principles that people can begin to see that there is more to life than profit.

Therefore, we see here that leadership can effect real change in the world:

> Conversion of life in this context does not mean a subjective 'conversion experience', but the gradual, dogged and determined conversion not only of one's own personal life, but the life of one's whole community and one's world.

This is pretty strong stuff. It indicates that leadership is a moral crusade or it's nothing.

Prayer and people

Benedict's rules are not about prayer, they're really about living together.

Those who don't work in ethical industries, or whose investors are from a similar provenance, don't have to compromise their principles. Balance is, under any circumstances, an ambition for all of us. It is so easily lost and yet needs to remain uppermost as an approach.

Benedictine thinking says much about modern leadership. For instance, the way of life involves equal time spent in prayer, reading and work. Of course, the proportions may be arbitrary, the lesson here is about balance. It was the Roman poet Ovid who said:

> Take rest; a field that has rested gives a bountiful crop.[14]

St Benedict is the patron saint of Europe and the father of Western civilization. Listening to this leadership thinking requires an open mind. It draws deep from the wells of Western wisdom. Its distilled wisdom in summary is that business specifically and our lives in general will be nurtured and grow not only more prosperous but more peaceful.

Professor Francis Davis is Professor of Religion, Communities and Public Policy at the University of Birmingham. He's also

Director of Policy at the Edward Cadbury Centre. He works at the intersection of business, civil society and central and local governments. 'The tradition of most business school finance modules is to behave like a seminary and teach only shareholder value as the unquestioned and undebated faith,' he says. 'This isn't to say that one should dump EBITDA, ROI and shareholder return, but that ideas of value in other areas can help leaders to think and develop habits. It also helps them identify sources of private equity, clients and collaborations where shared values lever more long-term returns than financial fixes at the outset.'[15]

The spirituality deficit

Davis says there are real problems when it comes to accepting the notion of spirituality in leadership: 'When it comes to spirituality we might freak thinking it sounds religious and then assume that we have to invent/find/buy in lots of resource when spirituality or reflexivity and resilience are to be found in our existing teams.' He points out that the reason for this is because people have never felt safe or encouraged to talk about it or explore how it could add to their work and purposefulness.

For instance, the finance leader who is so quiet but spends a couple of evenings and his weekends running life-transforming boxing or soccer for kids? He has to find the time, dig deep into resources to encourage, be a surrogate parent to some of them and a lifesaver to others. This, without doubt, shapes who he can be and how he can inspire at work.

Likewise, the woman in the project team who seems to have a low appetite for risk but goes free climbing at heights and snowboarding on the steepest slopes? There is spirituality in the sea and the mountains. Running and wild swimming require planning, resilience, paying close attention to particular elements and filtering out unnecessary detail.

Or the board member who never, ever speaks of the inner resources they had to find when their son spent three years doing heroin and the house kept being ransacked, or caring for their partner year after year after year as early onset dementia set in, or when they found their daughter had a cancer that required numerous hospital visits for tests.

Davis says that the biggest danger of all is not that we might bring spirituality into the workplace. That's already there, but 'because religious bodies have become so untrusted, we throw out the deeper wisdoms that transcend their failures'.

The Indian government gets this and has noticed that mindfulness is now a big export industry. Each Indian High Commission/ Embassy or an associated consulate now retains a specialist in mindfulness and meditation to embed related positive habits in the awareness of host countries.

Davis says that the LGBTQ movement has been really good at getting us to think about 'bringing our whole selves to work', 'but in so many places all this stuff (above) remains excluded and in effect excludes the very heart of much of who we are, who we could be and what we could do and be together, especially in those ventures which need constant (re)invention. It all ends up missing from our "*to be*" list.'

Of course, all of these things may be absent from an organization. If that's true, chances are you have a strategic competence gap in a fluid world – a spirituality/resilience/reflexive deficit that in the long run will mean your people can't cope with complexity or manage without hierarchy, or lead with energy that can be renewed, all of which are the order of the day.

Summary

Far from being a solution to the current problems, the way our education systems are configured is contributing significantly to leadership problems. The system's emphasis on individual achievement and grading runs counter to most collaborative work environments graduates will encounter. It promotes egocentricity and equates intellectual competence with workplace competence. Any employer of graduates will relate that many of the basic skills required for the workplace are often missing. Chief among these is experience of working with diverse groups, not by race or ethnicity but by age and cultural diversity. We believe the wholesale rejection of organized religion has resulted in the ejection of *baby and bathwater*. The essential message of spiritual balance remains an enduring and valuable contribution to the leadership debate.

This is not a call for a return to a more organized religion. It does, however, reflect the strong desire for balance that many feel. Religion is just one way of achieving this, so we shouldn't be sceptical about the motive for practising it. We all have the same requirement, but each of us has our own way of addressing it.

The question of balance and the infinite nature of that challenge to remain centred raises many overlapping issues, which need to be seen holistically. This is where we go next.

CHAPTER NINE

Where this thinking takes us

How can we summarize the benefits of balance and zero leadership? What do they look like? Is there such a thing as duty? Is it the same as responsibility or love? How can we apply it to the way we work right now? Can it inform our ability for strategic thought? Can it make us more successful?

We can see that balance has been an issue for recorded history. It is difficult to achieve, even harder to maintain. It is an infinite task. That doesn't mean it's not a suitable ambition for leadership. It's an attitude that is conspicuous by its absence in so many instances of leadership failure.

It may not maximize profits in the short term. It may not achieve the highest production targets. It may not leverage people to the highest capacity. It is, however, more durable, more sustainable and more efficient in the long term. How do we know this? Because it's been central to much of religious practice as regards work. The example of the Benedictines in the last chapter illustrates this more balanced approach.

How do we know this will happen? Because it's already happening with a new generation that expects and demands capital to behave better. This may not be what capital wants because it seeks the most efficient, leveraged use of people. We should never forget, however, that capital is our servant, not our master. Unless we harness it, it will harness us. This means that our overall vision must cover more than finance.

We should never forget that capital is our servant, not our master.

Leadership wields power, but authority resides elsewhere. It usually resides with the consent of another group. These might be customers, employees or voters. This is why community activation is an important element of consent because it leads to motivation levels that no commercial organization can touch. Take the Girl Scouts of America for instance. This organization reports high levels of donations and frequent cases of its supporters working harder than they would for monetary rewards. Their voluntary contributions are greater than any that could be achieved through compulsion alone. It's also illustrated throughout history. Community activation helped build Stone Age megaliths. It built Chartres Cathedral.[1] It created Wikipedia free of charge in a shorter time than it took Microsoft to spend millions on Encarta.[2]

Duty and responsibility

Defining the concept of duty in the 21st century is not easy. If obligations are felt at all, it is lightly and without the sense of community expectation that once prevailed. It remains an important concept. It is extant in commercial leadership as fiduciary duty and due diligence. It also resides in compliance and the wider subject of ethics. These have not always been the subjects of boardroom debate. If not in the boardroom, they almost certainly will be elsewhere.

Wherever you find people taking responsibility, you will find love in the form of duty. This applies especially to the family. The act of caring for a child or for an elderly parent is born out of love. Wherever you find responsibility you will find leadership. It starts with love. Leaders are positive and authentic. Leaders are having fun. Trump rallies. Leaders celebrate.

The four Hs of servant leadership

Responsibility is like authority. It's best taken, not given. It's something that people feel and it comes down to love. Love is about creating unity and holistic thinking. This is what's often talked about as servant leadership and it breaks out into the four Hs. Leadership that is humble, happy, honest and hungry.

Humble

This means someone who is happy not to take the credit and to encourage and develop and train others. Modesty and selflessness are at the core of this. It is an individual whose first thoughts are for the others in the community that they serve.

Happy

It is not the leader's job to make anyone happy. Each individual makes the choice whether to be happy or not. Some go in search of happiness, somehow conflating it with joy, when in reality it represents contentment.

Honest

This sounds like table stakes, but in most of the leadership failures we've discussed, honesty both with the community and with themselves has been an issue. Can you train people to be honest? No. You can, however, train leaders to recognize bias and avoid areas where they may become ethically conflicted.

Hungry

There's no point becoming a leader unless there are values to be defended and visions to be fulfilled. These need not be solely material goals. They could also represent the achievement of potential and individual development.

This sort of leadership is about the long term, but the average tenure of leaders is now five years.[3] This sort of leadership is about hope, just like politics. With faith in mainstream political parties reaching a low level, the leader of the organization now needs to represent the views of colleagues. This is leadership for all levels – leadership that speaks last. Leadership that is not as skilled as everyone else, but more trusted. Leadership that is about *being* something, not *doing* something. That has a 'to be' list. Not a 'to do' list. Leadership that *is* the love in the room.

The need for imagination and creativity

Leadership has the imagination to perceive the world in different ways. At the strategic level this level of imagination is at least as important as domain knowledge, experience or skill. Most leadership failure is not caused by a lack of knowledge and experience, but a lack of imagination is definitely a culprit. For instance, combating the threat of a rogue country is easier if you perceive that organized crime and the state are the same thing.

The need for strategic thinking

As seen in the education scorecard in Chapter 8, it's no accident that those qualities on the right might be described as softer skills. The quality that summarizes so many of the model's right-hand side qualities is 'sticking power'. This is not something you will find on any professional and managerial checklist. There is

FIGURE 9.1 The tactical vs strategic model

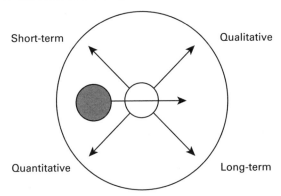

not a Myers–Briggs test for it, nor is there a DiSC score. But, there could be a zero model-based assessment.

We could apply axes on long-term versus short-term. These could be intercepted with quantitative and qualitative thinking (the action/goals model). See Figure 9.1.

We can apply the same methodology for this tactical vs strategic model.

The short term

This is defined as anything affecting the profit and loss account. Something that will be felt immediately. The odd thing about the short term is that it keeps getting shorter. Why the growth in short-term thinking? Nasdaq asks all its companies to report every 90 days. Each report is accompanied by a press release and earnings call, where analysts can question the company on its performance. Why would any long-term investor want this? Simple answer: trust. Investors have become so wary about losing their money (or maximizing it) that they want to know constantly what the company is doing. This, more than anything else, for stock market companies encourages short-term thinking. No one will notice if research and development or training are cut or marketing costs are brought down in the short term. Profits can be artificially manipulated to appear higher.

The long term

This is usually associated with the balance sheet of the company. It also protects the shareholders' long-term interests. It is called the balance sheet because whatever the company assets are long term, they must also have ownership. So a monetary asset always balances with a liability to ownership. This is why it is known as equity. It is the balancing item. A set of company accounts echoes the notion of a zero balance. With current assets equalling current liabilities and fixed assets equalling fixed liabilities. Items included in the long-term accounting of a company would include 'goodwill'. This is the intangible value of the company's reputation or values of its brand.

Quantitative

All leaders have a choice of ways to measure performance. They can be hard numbers such as revenues and expenses. They can be numbers that express ratios, eg the amount of cash in the business to cover immediate calls upon it. This is a ratio called 'the acid test', which in a healthy business is never less than 1:1 debt to cash. We might use quantitative measures to assess profit or revenue per head or costs per square foot of office space. We could also measure hard numbers longitudinally, ie comparing this year to prior years. This could then give more data about trends. These are all equally valid ways of measuring performance.

Qualitative

These are the softer measures that a leader uses. For example, the ability to 'read the room' or notice the expressions on people's faces. A good leader walks the floors and assesses the atmosphere. How well is good performance celebrated? How are inexperienced or junior staff treated? Is there an *esprit de corps*? How do teams react when presented with problems or extra work? The measure used here might be the phrases from exit interviews. It could be customer comments about service or the number of complaints. Cleanliness and tidiness are often used by experienced leaders. How much do people respect the working environment? How safe is it? How old and damaged is the office furniture? All of these factors might be considered to be qualitative measures.

The quadrants

In the same way as above, the 'cure' for overly short-term, quantitative leadership is the opposite diagonal quadrant.

The Scrooge zone (left)

Everyone can recognize environments that are run in the *Scrooge* style. These might be workplaces that require people to clock in. It could be shift work in a warehouse. Or where there are timed tea-breaks and staff benefits like sickness or medical cover are limited. This is typical of flexible employment contracts. Typically, these environments have low morale. They often feature low-skilled, transient or immigrant workforces. Equally, these could also be very high-value workplaces where considerable amounts can be earned, but the hours might be long and pressurized. The leadership is likely to be money-orientated and focused on little else, eg personal welfare.

The political zone (right)

Working with long-term qualitative goals, away from the short-term numbers, is rare but it's what you see being presented as political leadership. This 'feelgood leadership' is designed for the never-never.

FIGURE 9.2 The failure–success model

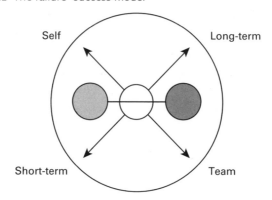

The palliative zone (upper)

In a similar way, it's far from obvious how things will be achieved in the short term, so the goal becomes mainly palliative – effectively pastoral care – to manage decline with the minimum of fuss.

The long haul (lower)

This is the quadrant where you see a long-term commitment to quantitative targets. It is where genuine strategic, verifiable change occurs. It can only happen if all parties are committed to long-term change.

We can also correlate selfish short-termism on a failure–success model (Figure 9.2). Successful leadership is almost always geared around team-based, long-term thinking. In other words, anyone can be successful in a one-off moment. Real leadership equates to success over time.

What does it take to lead?

You're here. That's a good indication of your leadership potential. Everyone has this, even highly experienced leaders. The very definition of leadership is the capacity to reinvent yourself to learn and develop your skills.

Curiosity

Curiosity is fundamental. Without this, leadership goes nowhere. It's not enough to understand other people, you have to understand yourself. The true definition of leadership is only revealed to the most experienced of leaders – that the true dawning of experience is humbling. You suddenly realize how much there still is to know. This is the beginning.

Ego (or lack thereof)

If you're not here for ego reasons, it helps. Leadership can never be about self-aggrandizement. Ego is kryptonite to team ethos, to use a reference to Superman's only point of vulnerability. The leader has primarily got to have the interests of others at heart. Whether it's being better as a matter of professionalism or because it's the right thing, it can never be about you. Leaders are the people you'll see doing anything to help, because leadership is not about the leader. It's about the 'ship'. If it helps to go get the coffee and bagels, then a real leader will do it. Sometimes, leaders won't do what they consider to be menial tasks. Ask yourself this though. How is it possible for wide groups of people to see your leadership potential if you don't? If being seen standing in the coffee shop would raise eyebrows, then good. Do it. Word will spread.

Energy

No leader goes anywhere without it. The energy can come in many forms. It can be mental, emotional, physical or spiritual. It can manifest itself as restlessness. It can be impatient. Every physicist knows that you cannot destroy energy, you can only change its form. Brakes can slow down a car, but they get hot as they do so. The best type of leadership energy is that which inspires, praises, reassures and encourages because that releases energy in the recipients. Note for the Type A 'to do' list merchants, you can't 'do' any of these, you can only 'be' them. A good leader can feel and read the energy in the room. Yet many of today's leaders don't even feel the pain in their own arm that presages an imminent heart attack, let alone have the capacity to discern how others are feeling. Most organizations have someone who has a deep understanding of such feelings. Some can feel what is happening to the people and the institution. It can be the leader but often it isn't.

Responsibility/duty/commitment

Some people just wouldn't feel right unless they volunteered. They would feel like they were letting the side down. Are you one of those? If so, you're a natural leader because you feel responsibility, so you take it. Wherever people take responsibility, you'll find leadership. These people are sometimes unaware of it, because they don't do it for gain. They do it because they just wouldn't feel right unless they did.

Love

At this stage, you might be asking 'the Tina Turner question' – What's love got to do with it? Love makes things grow. It makes the originator grow. It makes the recipient grow. To live a life without love is to have lived in black, white and grey rather than vivid colours. Love quickens the pulse and sharpens the senses. It fulfils. It is non-contingent. Love reaches out, unifies and joins things together. It sees the bigger picture. Love does not think. Love feels. It develops and nurtures. It puts out fires and quenches thirst. It nourishes and strengthens. It is consistent. It is persistent. It survives the grave and all religions are based upon it. Great leadership is founded on love. The love for one's colleagues. The love for the consequences of one's leadership decisions for others, rather than for the love of self. The love of life. The scientific and logical model has undermined this model in leadership and it needs to be corrected. It is OK to love what you do. It's not a sign of a failure or being a 'workaholic'. It's just important that this is balanced with a love of other things.

As anyone who has been in a long-term relationship knows, love is manifested mainly in small acts of regular kindness and support. In the team, this is constantly being ready to recognize imbalance and where support is needed. The leader's job is *not* to provide this support. The leader's job is to create a culture where this support is mutual among team members.

> *The leader's job is to create a culture where support is mutual among team members.*

Magic

The ability to create magic is a vital component of leadership. It is closely related to love because it confers the ability to render reality as malleable. Even the most intractable problems can be solved if we reframe them in a new way. We are not saying leaders can magic away problems. We are saying that a belief that magic can help solve problems is helpful. Magic can be seen when people enjoy their work, their team, their role. Magic is the ability to inspire and to motivate and change perceptions. It is not the gift of being the smartest person in the room. The leader's job is to make everyone else feel like they're the smartest person in the room. This is the leader's normative field. The magic is the intangible quality that reassures, that represents, that forgives and heals.

But what if I don't want to be a leader?

That's OK too, but whether you like it or not, at some stage leadership will come knocking at your door. Anyone that stands up for anything at any stage has to show leadership. This will come to you in parenting, in care for the elderly, in sports, in relationships, in the community as well as at work. You can't avoid it because leadership is coming right around the corner at you so you'd better be ready.

Do not confuse leadership with titles. We all know that the person with a title is not always the person in charge. Sometimes leadership comes from those who have no title but who really know what is going on, and everyone knows this.

Since ancient times, we have always recognized that some people are shamen or witch doctors. They do not lead. They do not judge. They do not arbitrate. But, when things get tough everyone trusts them to diagnose the problem, to find a way to reconcile conflicts and to bring out the best in people. Every organization has unrecognized shamen, 'go-to' people, firefighters, firelighters and community builders. Leaders could and should draw more on these quiet contributors to better outcomes. We should recognize the role they play in telling leaders what they need to hear instead of only what they want to hear. Others are magicians who some-how conjure forth the best in others. There are modern-day wizards who help leaders achieve better outcomes.

It is easy to dismiss these ideas as 'soft'. But that simply implies a belief that being 'hard' is correct. Yet hard-headed, rational leaders keep failing. One could dismiss magic and love too. Yet we all know great leaders whose essence was that the spells they cast had magic. Modern-day spells are literally spelt. This is why there is magic in slogans like Nike's 'Just Do It', Apple's 'Think Different' and L'Oréal's 'You're Worth It'. If we circle back through history we can see that magic derives from words. Leaders succeed better when there is enchant-ment in their words, their mission statements, their incantations. Think of Lincoln's 'Four score and seven years ago today'. Think of Kennedy's 'Ask not what your country can do for you, but what you can do for your country'. Some love Donald Trump's 'Make America Great Again' and some hate it.

Some may call him an example of zero leadership but he does manage to do much of what he says he will. But perhaps he is better thought of as a type of leadership – one that pushes things in a certain direction, often at the expense of specific interests. Will Donald Trump be remembered as a good leader or a bad one? How can we judge this best? How can we measure ourselves as well? This is a powerful and important question at this juncture in history. We think our model of zero leadership will provide a handy compass that will help guide us into a better future.

Let us just take a moment to remind ourselves – this is not a dress rehearsal.

Leadership is for everyone. Anyone can show it. Anyone can take responsibility. Leaders do not say 'it's not my responsibility'. By being a better leader, we can learn to choose better leaders, because we know what qualities to look for.

Somehow, we have come to believe that leadership is entertainment. It is not. Leaders are the people in whom we place collective responsibility and our mandated authority. The bearing of responsibility is not frivolous. You become a leader by taking responsibility. Real leadership is never given. It is earned. It's up to all of us to ensure that when our leaders take responsibility for us they do so with the *intent* of serving our long-term interests.

You become a leader by taking responsibility. Real leadership is never given. It is earned.

Summary

In ages past, our leaders recognized that we were at our best in moments like this. We've been on our own before. We've been on our own in the dark. We know that just ahead lies the hour of our greatest test. We can't change this overnight. The first step is to be aware of it.

In the darkness that surrounds us though, something is stirring, something ancient and timeless. Among our younger colleagues we see a new generation of leaders emerging. They are modern, pragmatic, technical and yes, they remain romantics. There is a new belief forming that with optimism, belief and love in our hearts, something very exciting and historic is about to happen.

Of course, you could ascribe this to the naivety of youth. You could say that, in time, they will become as cynical as everyone else. But what is cynicism, except a state of gross imbalance? We can see this everywhere in the ability to recognize, for instance, that the world is so much better, wealthier, happier, healthier and safer than it has ever been.

If we can achieve this, with the leadership problems we have, then what could be the potential for the future?

But to arrive at this magical place where we and our leaders are aligned, we have to understand the value and qualities of balance, and the idea that anything is possible, that infinite outcomes await us. This will replace our shame with pride and allow all of us to begin again to talk of the power of us.

Conclusions

This books calls for:

- a realization of the continuing problem of leadership failure and its reasons;
- leaders and their teams to see the problem of imbalance and its consequences;
- a recognition that this is an ongoing challenge, with lessons from the past;
- education reform that addresses the need for collaboration and cooperation;
- an understanding that this problem cannot be solved with analytical thinking alone;
- a new leadership model based on balance across intersecting criteria;
- a greater agility from leaders to balance demands of conflicting priorities;
- an awareness that imbalance manifests as injustice, waste and inefficiency;

- an end to the correlation of confidence with competence. They are not the same;
- a review of qualitative variables in assessing leadership performance;
- a capital model that encourages minimal capital and maximum collaboration;
- leadership development that embraces ethics, divinity, diversity and spirituality.

Notes

Introduction

1 https://www.poetryfoundation.org/poems/51642/invictus (archived at https://perma.cc/YY2X-7GLB)

2 Korczynski, M (2002) *Human Resource Management in Service Work*, 2001 edn, Palgrave, Basingstoke

3 ONS (nd) Services sector, UK: 2008 to 2018, Office for National Statistics, https://www.ons.gov.uk/economy/economicoutputandproductivity/output/articles/servicessectoruk/2008to2018 (archived at https://perma.cc/Y77V-RG6G)

4 OECD (2000) The Public Employment Service in the United States, Organisation for Economic Co-operation and Development, http://www.oecd.org/employment/emp/36867947.pdf (archived at https://perma.cc/392K-4669)

Chapter 1

1 Strategy& (nd) 2018 CEO Success Study, PwC, https://www.strategyand.pwc.com/gx/en/insights/ceo-success.html (archived at https://perma.cc/HVR9-K6EC)

2 Pressman, A (2017) How Apple uses the Channel Island of Jersey in tax strategy, *Fortune*, 6 November, http://fortune.com/2017/11/06/apple-tax-avoidance-jersey/ (archived at https://perma.cc/LXL9-QZWW)

3 Carrington, D (2015) Four more carmakers join diesel emissions row, *Guardian*, 9 October, https://www.theguardian.com/environment/2015/oct/09/mercedes-honda-mazda-mitsubishi-diesel-emissions-row (archived at https://perma.cc/B9WJ-GER9)

4 Ridley, K and Freifeld, K (2015) Deutsche Bank fined record $2.5 billion over rate rigging, *Reuters*, 23 April, https://www.reuters.com/article/us-deutschebank-libor-settlement/deutsche-bank-fined-record-2-5-billion-over-rate-rigging-idUSKBN0NE12U20150423 (archived at https://perma.cc/AH75-EYUR)

5 Rushe, D (2012) HSBC 'sorry' for aiding Mexican drugs lords, rogue states and terrorists, *Guardian*, 17 July, https://www.theguardian.com/business/2012/jul/17/hsbc-executive-resigns-senate (archived at https://perma.cc/29Q9-2MPD)

6 Rapoza, K (2017) Tax haven cash rising, now equal to at least 10% of world GDP, *Forbes*, 15 September, https://www.forbes.com/sites/kenrapoza/2017/09/15/tax-haven-cash-rising-now-equal-to-at-least-10-of-world-gdp/#572b443f70d6 (archived at https://perma.cc/E8EX-LGY4)

7 Treanor, J (2016) RBS facing £400m bill to compensate small business customers, *Guardian*, 8 November, https://www.theguardian.com/business/2016/nov/08/rbs-facing-400m-bill-to-compensate-small-business-customers (archived at https://perma.cc/8A3C-NQKB)

8 Cumbo, J (2017) MPs raise concerns over 'brewing pensions scandal', *Financial Times*, 27 October, https://www.ft.com/content/87f72e9e-bafb-11e7-9bfb-4a9c83ffa852 (archived at https://perma.cc/K95N-43KU)

9 Mathiason, N (2008) Three weeks that changed the world, *Guardian*, 28 December, https://www.theguardian.com/business/2008/dec/28/markets-credit-crunch-banking-2008 (archived at https://perma.cc/Q2EY-WD9E)

10 Yang, S (2014) 5 years ago Bernie Madoff was sentenced to 150 years in prison – here's how his scheme worked, *Business Insider*, 1 July, http://www.businessinsider.com/how-bernie-madoffs-ponzi-scheme-worked-2014-7 (archived at https://perma.cc/X5NP-K6KW)

11 Park, M (2017) Timeline: a look at the Catholic Church's sex abuse scandals, *CNN*, 29 June, https://www.cnn.com/2017/06/29/world/timeline-catholic-church-sexual-abuse-scandals/index.html (archived at https://perma.cc/8G8N-S9T2)

12 BBC (2018) Oxfam Haiti scandal: thousands cancel donations to charity, BBC News, 20 February, http://www.bbc.co.uk/news/uk-43121833 (archived at https://perma.cc/KTL8-B7ZX)

13 BBC (2020) Harvey Weinstein timeline: how the scandal unfolded, BBC News, 29 May, http://www.bbc.co.uk/news/entertainment-arts-41594672 (archived at https://perma.cc/Q2UF-WEHN)

14 Greenslade, R (2014) Newsnight's McAlpine scandal – 13 days that brought down the BBC's chief, *Guardian*, 19 February, https://www.theguardian.com/media/greenslade/2014/feb/19/newsnight-lord-mcalpine (archived at https://perma.cc/7SXE-73T5)

15 Watson, L, Ward, V and Foster, P (2016) 'Atmosphere of fear' at BBC allowed Jimmy Savile to commit sex crimes, report finds, *Telegraph*, 25 February, https://www.telegraph.co.uk/news/uknews/crime/jimmy-savile/12172773/Jimmy-Savile-sex-abuse-report-to-be-published-live.html (archived at https://perma.cc/9WKW-VBNV)

16 BBC (2018) Russia doping: country still suspended by IAAF and could face permanent ban, BBC Sport, 6 March, http://www.bbc.co.uk/sport/athletics/43301116 (archived at https://perma.cc/C3AH-5XVT)

17 Campbell, D (2013) Mid Staffs hospital scandal: the essential guide, *Guardian*, 6 February, https://www.theguardian.com/society/2013/feb/06/mid-staffs-hospital-scandal-guide (archived at https://perma.cc/6XJZ-B6JT)

18 Busby, M (2018) How many of Donald Trump's advisers have been convicted? *Guardian*, 14 September, https://www.theguardian.com/us-news/2018/aug/22/how-many-of-trumps-close-advisers-have-been-convicted-and-who-are-they (archived at https://perma.cc/34VY-7P2M)

19 Scharfenberg, D (2018) Trillions of dollars have sloshed into offshore tax havens. Here's how to get it back, *Boston Globe*, 20 January, https://www.bostonglobe.com/ideas/2018/01/20/trillions-dollars-have-sloshed-into-offshore-tax-havens-here-how-get-back/2wQAzH5DGRw0mFH0YPqKZJ/story.html (archived at https://perma.cc/JT33-R4AA)

20 Desjardins, J (2018) The $80 trillion world economy in one chart, *Visual Capitalist*, 10 October, https://www.visualcapitalist.com/80-trillion-world-economy-one-chart/ (archived at https://perma.cc/P34K-2G97)

21 Lahart, J (2009) Mr Rajan was unpopular (but prescient) at Greenspan party, *New York Times*, 2 January, https://www.wsj.com/articles/SB123086154114948151 (archived at https://perma.cc/2562-W7VG)

22 United Nations (2020) This is how much the coronavirus will cost the world's economy, according to the UN, *World Economic Forum*, 17 March, https://www.weforum.org/agenda/2020/03/coronavirus-covid-19-cost-economy-2020-un-trade-economics-pandemic/ (archived at https://perma.cc/ML36-AK36)

23 Le Fort, B (2018) The financial crisis cost the US economy $22 trillion, *Impact Economics*, 4 October, https://medium.com/impact-economics/the-financial-crisis-cost-the-u-s-economy-22-trillion-440b6d9b6313 (archived at https://perma.cc/M3AT-JGSH)

24 FRBSF (2018) The financial crisis at 10: will we ever recover? Federal Reserve Bank of San Francisco, Economic Letter, 13 August, https://www.frbsf.org/economic-research/publications/economic-letter/2018/august/financial-crisis-at-10-years-will-we-ever-recover/ (archived at https://perma.cc/F9SW-E6V7)

25 GAO (2013) Financial regulatory reform: financial crisis losses and potential impacts of the Dodd–Frank Act, United States Government Accountability Office, January, https://www.gao.gov/assets/660/651322.pdf (archived at https://perma.cc/TMH5-Y4S7)

26 Chappell, B (2019) US national debt hits record $22 trillion, *NPR*, 13 February, https://www.npr.org/2019/02/13/694199256/u-s-national-debt-hits-22-trillion-a-new-record-thats-predicted-to-fall (archived at https://perma.cc/7QJM-5T22)

27 https://en.wikipedia.org/wiki/United_States_federal_budget#/media/File:2018_Federal_Budget_Infographic.png (archived at https://perma.cc/JJJ5-7WGQ)

28 https://en.wikipedia.org/wiki/Budget_of_the_United_Kingdom (archived at https://perma.cc/X6SR-BLNM)

29 Curtin, M (2020) 94 percent of Millennials say this is their no 1 life goal (it's not career or love), *Inc*, 25 January, https://www.inc.com/melanie-curtin/94-percent-of-millennials-say-this-is-their-no-1-life-goal-its-not-career-or-love.html (archived at https://perma.cc/Z58F-KKQQ)

30 Hughes, A and Van Kessel, P (2018) 'Anger' topped 'love' when Facebook users reacted to lawmakers' posts after 2016 election, Pew Research Center, 18 July, https://www.pewresearch.org/fact-tank/2018/07/18/anger-topped-love-facebook-after-2016-election/ (archived at https://perma.cc/HL46-9B9H)

31 https://www.urbandictionary.com/define.php?term=Recreational%20Outrage (archived at https://perma.cc/ZJ8E-7WUK)

32 https://www.urbandictionary.com/define.php?term=Virtue%20Signalling (archived at https://perma.cc/4XR2-AB39)

33 RCN (2018) Violence and aggression in the NHS: estimating the size and the impact of the problem, Royal College of Nursing, https://www.rcn.org.uk/professional-development/publications/pub-007301 (archived at https://perma.cc/HJ8E-U4C4)

34 Adams, R (2019) One in four teachers 'experience violence from pupils every week', *Guardian*, 20 April, https://www.theguardian.com/education/2019/apr/20/one-in-four-teachers-experience-violence-from-pupils-every-week (archived at https://perma.cc/ZE87-SYES)

35 https://www.angermanage.co.uk/anger-statistics/ (archived at https://perma.cc/6JKC-H2Y5)

36 IATA (2016) Collaboration needed to stem unruly passenger incidents, International Air Transport Association, 28 September, http://www.iata.org/pressroom/pr/Pages/2016-09-28-01.aspx (archived at https://perma.cc/Y5XJ-BVWC)

37 https://www.angermanage.co.uk/anger-statistics/ (archived at https://perma.cc/6JKC-H2Y5)

38 https://www.angermanage.co.uk/anger-statistics/ (archived at https://perma.cc/6JKC-H2Y5)

39 Gallup (2019) Gallup Global Emotions Report, https://www.gallup.com/analytics/248906/gallup-global-emotions-report-2019.aspx (archived at https://perma.cc/E9Q2-AZ4R)

40 https://en.wikipedia.org/wiki/The_Lehman_Trilogy (archived at https://perma.cc/2B8T-CV77)

41 https://en.wikipedia.org/wiki/Enron_(play) (archived at https://perma.cc/3B3G-HZMQ)

42 Sorkin, A R (2010) *Too Big to Fail: The inside story of how Wall Street and Washington fought to save the financial system – and themselves*, Penguin, New York, NY

43 Tooze, A (2019) *Crashed: How a decade of financial crises changed the world*, Penguin, New York, NY

44 Ahamed, L (2009) *Lords of Finance: The bankers who broke the world*, Penguin, New York, NY

45 McLean, B and Nocera, J (2011) *All the Devils Are Here: The hidden history of the financial crisis*, Portfolio/Penguin, New York, NY

46 Roubini, N and Mihm, S (2011) *Crisis Economics: A crash course in the future of finance*, Penguin, New York, NY

47 Foroohar, R (2017) *Makers and Takers: How Wall Street destroyed Main Street*, Crown Business, New York, NY

48 Lowenstein, R (2011) *The End of Wall Street*, Penguin, New York, NY

49 Farrell, G (2010) *Crash of the Titans: Greed, hubris, the fall of Merrill Lynch, and the near-collapse of Bank of America*, Crown Business, New York, NY

50 https://www.imdb.com/title/tt1596363/ (archived at https://perma.cc/PNZ2-WLMB)

51 https://www.imdb.com/title/tt5865326/ (archived at https://perma.cc/QZ3Y-F2W6)

52 https://quoteinvestigator.com/2010/12/04/good-men-do/ (archived at https://perma.cc/UA22-Q6CB)

53 Kübler-Ross, E, Kessler, D and Shriver, M (2014) *On Grief and Grieving: Finding the meaning of grief through the five stages of loss*, Scribner, New York, NY

54 Eatwell, R and Goodwin, M (2018) *National Populism: The revolt against liberal democracy*, Pelican, London

55 Reeves, J A (2011) *The Road to Somewhere: An American memoir*, W W Norton & Company, New York, NY

56 Doherty, C (2017) Key takeaways on Americans' growing partisan divide over political values, Pew Research Center, 5 October, https://www.pewresearch.org/fact-tank/2017/10/05/takeaways-on-americans-growing-partisan-divide-over-political-values/ (archived at https://perma.cc/V97H-PTXQ)

57 https://www.goodreads.com/quotes/63219-the-children-now-love-luxury-they-have-bad-manners-contempt (archived at https://perma.cc/83F7-S5EQ)

58 Kolirin, L (2019) Royal Shakespeare Company cuts ties with BP after school students threaten boycott, *CNN*, 2 October, https://www.cnn.com/style/article/rsc-bp-ends-gbr-scli-intl/index.html (archived at https://perma.cc/8XCM-LJLZ)

59 Templafy (2017) How many emails are sent every day? Top email statistics for business, *Templafy*, September, https://info.templafy.com/blog/how-many-emails-are-sent-every-day-top-email-statistics-your-business-needs-to-know (archived at https://perma.cc/UM6K-L853)

60 Sorokin, S (2019) Thriving in a world of 'knowledge half-life', *CIO*, 5 April, https://www.cio.com/article/3387637/thriving-in-a-world-of-knowledge-half-life.html (archived at https://perma.cc/C9GN-85NK)

61 https://www.reddit.com/r/singularity/comments/8ksckm/any_recent_estimates_for_where_we_are_on_the/ (archived at https://perma.cc/FN5C-2JC6)

62 McLuhan, M (2011) *The Gutenberg Galaxy*, updated edn, University of Toronto Press, Toronto

63 Quinn, J (2008) Greenspan admits mistakes in 'once in a century credit tsunami', *Telegraph*, 23 October, https://www.telegraph.co.uk/finance/financialcrisis/3248774/Greenspan-admits-mistakes-in-once-in-a-century-credit-tsunami.html (archived at https://perma.cc/JBW3-EWTG)

64 https://www.imdb.com/title/tt1596363/ (archived at https://perma.cc/PNZ2-WLMB)

65 https://quoteinvestigator.com/2017/11/30/salary/ (archived at https://perma.cc/E2A8-ZAVA)

66 De Tocqueville, A (2013) *Democracy in America and Two Essays on America*, Penguin Classics, London

67 Gladwell, M (2009) *Outliers: The story of success*, Penguin, London

68 Chamorro-Premuzic, T (2013) Why do so many incompetent men become leaders? *Harvard Business Review*, 22 August, https://www.5050foundation.edu.au/assets/reports/documents/Why-Do-So-Many-Incompetent-Men-Become-Leaders.pdf (archived at https://perma.cc/6PG2-KQCX)

69 Beard, A (2018) *Natural Born Learners: Our incredible capacity to learn and how we can harness it*, Weidenfeld & Nicolson, London

70 Barnwell, P (2014) My students don't know how to have a conversation, *The Atlantic*, 22 April, https://www.theatlantic.com/education/archive/2014/04/my-students-dont-know-how-to-have-a-conversation/360993/ (archived at https://perma.cc/QA6F-64MV)

71 http://www.quotationspage.com/quote/23675.html (archived at https://perma.cc/9DZT-SNPQ)

72 http://www.asc.ox.ac.uk/person/46 (archived at https://perma.cc/S8FT-A7SN)

73 Beard, A (2018) *Natural Born Learners: Our incredible capacity to learn and how we can harness it*, Weidenfeld & Nicolson, London

74 Pink, D H (2018) *Drive: The surprising truth about what motivates us*, Canongate Books, Edinburgh

75 Crawford, M (2010) *The Case for Working With Your Hands: Or why office work is bad for us and fixing things feels good*, Penguin Books, London

76 Goodhart, D (2017) *The Road to Somewhere: The populist revolt and the future of politics*, Hurst & Company, London

Chapter 2

1 https://www.lexico.com/definition/magic (archived at https://perma.cc/ K4A4-VAPF)

2 Obringer, L A (2006) How the Navy SEALs work, *HowStuffWorks.com*, 27 November, https://science.howstuffworks.com/navy-seal7.htm (archived at https://perma.cc/K6VQ-6LH2)

3 Greitens, E (2012) *The Heart and the Fist*, Mariner Books, Boston, MA

4 https://iass-ais.org/dictionary-of-symbolism/ (archived at https://perma.cc/ P3MN-G8BJ)

5 http://umich.edu/~umfandsf/symbolismproject/symbolism.html/C/circle.html (archived at https://perma.cc/D4MX-4U6F)

6 Lima, M (2017) *The Book of Circles: Visualizing spheres of knowledge*, Princeton Architectural Press, New York, NY

7 Sneed, A (2016) Why the shape of a company's logo matters, *Fast Company*, 1 February, https://www.fastcompany.com/3056130/why-the-shape-of-a-companys-logo-matters (archived at https://perma.cc/4MFH-2WXY)

8 Chattopadhyay, A (2014) Logos mean more than you think, *Knowledge*, 1 August, https://iass-ais.org/dictionary-of-symbolism/ (archived at https://perma. cc/P3MN-G8BJ)

9 Murray, G R (2011) Do we really prefer taller leaders? *Psychology Today*, 14 November, https://www.psychologytoday.com/us/blog/caveman-politics/201111/ do-we-really-prefer-taller-leaders (archived at https://perma.cc/3T7Y-V7FU)

Chapter 3

1 Wood, G (2002) First chapter: *Edison's Eve* 25 August, https://www.nytimes. com/2002/08/25/books/chapters/edisons-eve.html (archived at https://perma.cc/ CG7W-36WK)

2 Seife, C (2000) *Zero: The biography of a dangerous idea*, Souvenir Press, London

3 Goldsmith, S B (2011) *Principles of Health Care Management: Foundations for a changing health care system*, 2nd edn, Jones and Bartlett Publishers, Boston, MA

4 Herzberg, F (2008) *One More Time: How do you motivate employees?* Harvard Business School Press, Boston, MA

5 Senge, P M (2006) *The Fifth Discipline: The art & practice of the learning organization*, Doubleday, New York, NY

6 McGregor, D (2006) *The Human Side of Enterprise*, annotated edn, McGraw-Hill, New York, NY

7 https://www.glofox.com/blog/10-gym-membership-statistics-you-need-to-know/ (archived at https://perma.cc/LC98-AYJN)

8 Dixon, M (nd) Soul Hypercycle and the wave of new fitness boutiques, *Toptal*, https://www.toptal.com/finance/equity-research-analysts/fitness-boutiques (archived at https://perma.cc/2TFQ-N3MP)

9 Weir, K (2012) What you need to know about willpower: the psychological science of self-control, American Psychological Association, https://www.apa.org/helpcenter/willpower (archived at https://perma.cc/SB7U-FBQU)

10 Carli, J (2018) Remembrance for Walter Mischel, psychologist who devised the marshmallow test, *NPR*, 21 September, https://www.npr.org/sections/health-shots/2018/09/21/650015068/remembrance-for-walter-mischel-psychologist-who-devised-the-marshmallow-test (archived at https://perma.cc/RK2X-ZXLU)

11 Tangney, J (2004) High self-control predicts good adjustment, less pathology, better grades, and interpersonal success, April, http://citeseerx.ist.psu.edu/viewdoc/download?doi=10.1.1.613.6909&rep=rep1&type=pdf (archived at https://perma.cc/V7ES-9DDC)

12 Bates, K L (2011) Childhood self-control predicts health and wealth, 24 January, https://today.duke.edu/2011/01/selfcontrol.html (archived at https://perma.cc/AJJ5-XAMF)

13 Baumeister, R F and Tierney, J (2012) *Willpower: Why self-control is the secret to success*, Penguin Books, London

14 Dostoevsky, F (1997) *Winter Notes on Summer Impressions*, tr David Patterson, Northwestern University Press, Evanston, IL

15 https://www.yourhormones.info/hormones/ghrelin/ (archived at https://perma.cc/FBT3-C6B4)

16 NPR/TED (2015) Why do we need sleep? *NPR*, 17 April, http://www.npr.org/2015/04/17/399800134/why-do-we-need-sleep (archived at https://perma.cc/75SX-T4KH)

17 Muraven, M, Gagné, M and Rosman, H (2008) Helpful self-control: autonomy support, vitality, and depletion, *Journal of Experimental Social Psychology*, 44 (3), pp 573–85

Chapter 4

1 I am indebted to Professor Russell Foster of Oxford University for this phrase

2 Pink, D H (2018) *Drive: The surprising truth about what motivates us*, Canongate Books, Edinburgh

3 https://www.angermanage.co.uk/anger-statistics/ (archived at https://perma.cc/6JKC-H2Y5)

4   Kaul, V (2011) The necktie syndrome: why CEOs tend to be significantly taller than the average male, *The Economic Times*, 30 September, https://economictimes.indiatimes.com/the-necktie-syndrome-why-ceos-tend- to-be-significantly-taller-than-the-average-male/articleshow/10178115.cms (archived at https://perma.cc/VC39-767T)

5   Schmidt, E (2019) *Trillion Dollar Coach: The leadership handbook of Silicon Valley's Bill Campbell*, John Murray, London

6   In conversation with Pippa Malmgren, Jonathan Rosenberg and Alan Eagle at the How To Academy on 13 May 2019.

7   Bryant, J H (2009) *Love Leadership: The new way to lead in a fear-based world*, Jossey-Bass, San Francisco, CA

8   MindTools (nd) 5 Whys: getting to the root of a problem quickly, MindTools, https://www.mindtools.com/pages/article/newTMC_5W.htm (archived at https://perma.cc/TMB9-E9KH)

9   Lewis, C (2016) *Too Fast to Think: How to reclaim your creativity in a hyper-connected work culture*, Kogan Page, London

10 Julian, K (2018) Why are young people having so little sex? *The Atlantic*, December, https://www.theatlantic.com/magazine/archive/2018/12/the-sex-recession/573949/ (archived at https://perma.cc/6F54-UAYP)

11 Business Insider (2016) 16 percent of people met their spouse at work, Business Insider, 13 February, https://www.businessinsider.com/surprising-office-romance-statistics-2016-2?r=US&IR=T (archived at https://perma.cc/V3TB-3VNS)

12 Thottam, I (nd) 10 online dating statistics you should know, eharmony, https://www.eharmony.com/online-dating-statistics/ (archived at https://perma.cc/AY2J-H227)

13 Stone, J (2014) Understanding impatience, *Psychology Today*, 4 November, https://www.psychologytoday.com/gb/blog/clear-organized-and-motivated/201411/understanding-impatience (archived at https://perma.cc/8XLL-6HFE)

14 ONS (2018) Population estimates by marital status and living arrangements, England and Wales: 2002 to 2017, Office for National Statistics, 27 July, https://www.ons.gov.uk/peoplepopulationandcommunity/population-andmigration/populationestimates/bulletins/populationestimatesbymaritalstatus andlivingarrangements/2002to2017 (archived at https://perma.cc/Z59S-ZY5H)

Chapter 5

1   Pendry, J D (2001) *The Three Meter Zone: Common sense leadership for NCOs*, Presidio Press, Novato, CA

2   McLeod, S (2017) The Milgram Shock Experiment, *SimplyPsychology*, https://www.simplypsychology.org/milgram.html (archived at https://perma. cc/6PVN-5H8P)

3   Csikszentmihalyi, M (2002) *Flow: The psychology of happiness*, Rider, London

4   Sorrel, C (2016) The bicycle is still a scientific mystery: here's why, *Fast Company*, 1 August, https://www.fastcompany.com/3062239/the-bicycle-is-still-a-scientific-mystery-heres-why (archived at https://perma.cc/MD3L-2W3D)

5   Herbert, K (1997) *Peace-Weavers and Shield Maidens: Women in early English society*, Anglo-Saxon Books, Ely

6   Daley, J (2020) Sneering liberals' contempt for ordinary people is the real issue facing post-Brexit Britain, *Telegraph*, 1 February, https://www.telegraph.co.uk/ politics/2020/02/01/sneering-liberals-contempt-ordinary-people-real-issue-facing/?utm_content=telegraph&utm_medium=Social&utm_campaign= Echobox&utm_source=Twitter#Echobox=1581770703 (archived at https:// perma.cc/4Z6A-CAE3)

7   https://quotefancy.com/quote/1574822/Fred-Emery-Instead-of-constantly-adapting-to-change-why-not-change-to-be-adaptive (archived at https://perma. cc/5MK7-4BYJ)

8   https://quotes.thefamouspeople.com/oliver-wendell-holmes-jr-2480.php (archived at https://perma.cc/MPJ6-8BEF)

9   https://www.goodreads.com/author/quotes/22302.Frank_Zappa (archived at https://perma.cc/U422-6J78)

10 Stephenson, S (2017) The duality of balanced leadership, *Forbes*, 29 November, https://www.forbes.com/sites/scottstephenson/2017/11/29/the-duality-of-balanced-leadership/#44320dff262d (archived at https://perma.cc/UAY9-NNWC)

11 https://www.goodreads.com/quotes/122468-the-world-is-full-of-magic-things-patiently-waiting-for (archived at https://perma.cc/VT7E-ZDQM)

12 Orwell, G (2004) *Nineteen Eighty-Four*, new edn (Penguin Modern Classics), Penguin Books, London

13 Poggioli, S (2014) Archaeologists unearth what may be oldest Roman temple, *NPR*, 29 January, https://www.npr.org/2014/01/29/267819402/archaeologists-unearth-what-may-be-oldest-roman-temple (archived at https://perma.cc/ NC8F-2EYP)

14 Jacobs, T (2017) The creativity of the wandering mind, *Pacific Standard*, 14 June, https://psmag.com/social-justice/the-creativity-of-the-wandering-mind-46242 (archived at https://perma.cc/3PDG-DWDL)

15 Powell, A J (2018) Mind and spirit: hypnagogia and religious experience, *The Lancet*, 5 April, https://www.thelancet.com/journals/lanpsy/article/PIIS2215-0366(18)30138-X/fulltext (archived at https://perma.cc/28Y6-65HX)

16 Descartes, R (2001) *Discourse on Method, Optics, Geometry, and Meteorology*, rev edn, tr P J Olscamp, Hackett Publishing Company, Indianapolis, IN

17 Dowbiggin, I (1990) Alfred Maury and the politics of the unconscious in nineteenth-century France, *History of Psychiatry*, 1 (3), pp 255–87

Chapter 6

1 Business Wire (2019) Woman-owned businesses are growing 2x faster on average than all businesses nationwide, Business Wire, 23 September, https://www.businesswire.com/news/home/20190923005500/en/Woman-Owned-Businesses-Growing-2X-Faster-Average-Businesses (archived at https://perma.cc/9NZ2-2BEW)

2 Hannon, K and Next Avenue (2018) Black women entrepreneurs: the good and not-so-good news, *Forbes*, 9 September, https://www.forbes.com/sites/nextavenue/2018/09/09/black-women-entrepreneurs-the-good-and-not-so-good-news/#322bd2a66ffe (archived at https://perma.cc/WA67-SMLP)

3 Azevedo, M A (2019) Untapped opportunity: minority founders still being overlooked, *Crunchbase News*, 27 February, https://news.crunchbase.com/news/untapped-opportunity-minority-founders-still-being-overlooked/ (archived at https://perma.cc/FZ5A-PFND)

4 Li, Y (2019) Don't be fooled by the 'unicorn' hype this year, most IPOs lose money for investors after 5 years, *CNBC*, 3 April, https://www.cnbc.com/2019/04/03/dont-be-fooled-by-the-unicorn-hype-this-year-most-ipos-lose-money-for-investors-after-5-years.html (archived at https://perma.cc/7NYA-4WKS)

5 The Daily (2019) The spectacular rise and fall of WeWork, *The Daily* (podcast), 18 November, https://www.nytimes.com/2019/11/18/podcasts/the-daily/wework-adam-neumann.html (archived at https://perma.cc/QY4J-DSWU)

6 Widdicombe, L (2019) The rise and fall of WeWork: employees look back on a wild ride in Unicornland, *New Yorker*, 6 November, https://www.newyorker.com/culture/culture-desk/the-rise-and-fall-of-wework (archived at https://perma.cc/GJP7-RHXE)

7 Chang, E (2018) *Brotopia: Breaking up the boys' club of Silicon Valley*, Portfolio, New York, NY

8 Chang, E (2018) 'Oh my god, this is so f...ed up': inside Silicon Valley's secretive, orgiastic dark side, *Vanity Fair*, 2 January, https://www.vanityfair.com/news/2018/01/brotopia-silicon-valley-secretive-orgiastic-inner-sanctum (archived at https://perma.cc/8NFU-KGXG)

9 Sieghart, M A (2019) How to fix the shocking, sexist collapse of female coders: today coding is dominated by men – but it hasn't always been this way, *Wired*, 1 April, https://www.wired.co.uk/article/women-in-computer-programming (archived at https://perma.cc/XNJ9-3BN6)

10 https://www.documentcloud.org/documents/3914586-Googles-Ideological-Echo-Chamber.html (archived at https://perma.cc/J6RX-5JL4)

11 Dean, T (2017) The meeting that showed me the truth about VCs, *TechCrunch*, 1 June, https://techcrunch.com/2017/06/01/the-meeting-that-showed-me-the-truth-about-vcs/ (archived at https://perma.cc/ET9V-HN6Q)

12 Williamson, S and Mirchandani, B (2019) What Beyond Meat and WeWork can teach us about the next decade of IPO investing, *CNBC*, 27 December, https://www.cnbc.com/2019/12/26/what-beyond-meat-wework-teach-us-about-ipos-of-next-decade.html (archived at https://perma.cc/4G63-DSBU)

13 SBA (2019) Small businesses drive job growth in United States; they account for 1.8 million net new jobs, latest data show, Office of Advocacy, 24 April, https://advocacy.sba.gov/2019/04/24/small-businesses-drive-job-growth-in-united-states-they-account-for-1-8-million-net-new-jobs-latest-data-show/ (archived at https://perma.cc/AYC9-WRUJ)

14 https://twitter.com/alvinfoo/status/1210645555447128064?s=20 (archived at https://perma.cc/8CPV-6ZQ6)

15 Mavadiya, M (2019) Why is Apple more trusted than Google? *Forbes*, 29 November 29, https://www.forbes.com/sites/madhvimavadiya/2019/11/29/why-is-apple-trusted-more-than-google/#556dde370878 (archived at https://perma.cc/SC6H-VUGS)

16 Pinker, S (2012) *The Better Angels of Our Nature: A history of violence and humanity*, Penguin Books, London

17 Diamandis, P H and Kotler, S (2012) *Abundance: The future is better than you think*, Free Press, New York, NY

18 Rosling, H, Rosling, O and Rosling Rönnlund, A (2018) *Factfulness: Ten reasons we're wrong about the world – and why things are better than you think*, Flatiron Books, New York, NY

19 https://www.econlib.org/library/Columns/LevyPeartdismal.html (archived at https://perma.cc/8NTC-ST4C)

20 https://www.intel.com/content/www/us/en/silicon-innovations/moores-law-technology.html (archived at https://perma.cc/Z9GC-HP9H)

21 Hoque, F (2012) Why most venture-backed companies fail, *Fast Company*, 10 December, https://www.fastcompany.com/3003827/why-most-venture-backed-companies-fail (archived at https://perma.cc/9Q7U-VYY9)

22 Otar, C (2018) What percentage of small businesses fail – and how can you avoid being one of them? *Forbes*, 25 October, https://www.forbes.com/sites/forbesfinancecouncil/2018/10/25/what-percentage-of-small-businesses-fail-and-how-can-you-avoid-being-one-of-them/#6f04f48443b5 (archived at https://perma.cc/V2NV-8ZP5)

23 https://www.umsl.edu/~sauterv/analysis/Fall2013Papers/Purcell/bucky.html (archived at https://perma.cc/LC7K-CKGD)

24 Haskel, J and Westlake, S (2017) *Capitalism Without Capital: The rise of the intangible economy*, Princeton University Press, Princeton, NJ

25 Gates, B (2018) Not enough people are paying attention to this economic trend: *Capitalism Without Capital* explains how things we can't touch are reshaping the economy, *GatesNotes*, 14 August, https://www.gatesnotes.com/Books/Capitalism-Without-Capital (archived at https://perma.cc/5SCW-YN49)

26 McAfee, A (2019) *More from Less: The surprising story of how we learned to prosper using fewer resources – and what happens next*, Scribner, New York, NY

27 Reday-Mulvey, G (1977) *The Potential for Substituting Manpower for Energy: Final report 30 July 1977 for the Commission of the European Communities*, Batelle, Geneva Research Centre

28 http://www.product-life.org/en/major-publications/the-product-life-factor (archived at https://perma.cc/2ASQ-GA6E)

29 https://www.sciencedirect.com/topics/agricultural-and-biological-sciences/cradle-to-grave (archived at https://perma.cc/A4AB-L37F)

30 Hansen, K (2012) The Cradle to Cradle concept in detail, *YouTube*, 21 March [video] https://www.youtube.com/watch?v=HM20zk8WvoM&list=ULPhJ-YZwDAVo&index=124 (archived at https://perma.cc/GH4Z-RAP3)

31 Herman, R, Ardekani, S A and Ausbel, J (1990) Dematerialization, *Technological Forecasting and Social Change*, 38, pp 333–47

32 Foxley, W (2019) President Xi says China should 'seize opportunity' to adopt blockchain, *Coindesk*, 25 October, https://www.coindesk.com/president-xi-says-china-should-seize-opportunity-to-adopt-blockchain (archived at https://perma.cc/6K78-K49K)

33 https://orpheusnyc.org/ (archived at https://perma.cc/CLP7-DGP5)

34 Matyszczyk, C (2017) The new Church of the AI God is even creepier than I imagined, *CNET*, 16 November, https://www.cnet.com/news/the-new-church-of-ai-god-is-even-creepier-than-i-imagined/ (archived at https://perma.cc/GL7C-MWS4)

35 Harris, M (2017) Inside the First Church of Artificial Intelligence: the engineer at the heart of the Uber/Waymo lawsuit is serious about his AI religion. Welcome to Anthony Levandowski's Way of the Future, *Wired*, 15 November, https://www.wired.com/story/anthony-levandowski-artificial-intelligence-religion/ (archived at https://perma.cc/XH2F-RGL9)

36 https://en.wikipedia.org/wiki/2010%E2%80%9311_Belgian_government_formation (archived at https://perma.cc/QC5H-JFF3)

37 https://winstonchurchill.org/the-life-of-churchill/life/artist/painting-as-a-pastime/ (archived at https://perma.cc/B9DC-B3ZT)

38 https://www.pocketmindfulness.com/no-leaders-please-charles-bukowski/ (archived at https://perma.cc/ASY4-M5QG)

39 https://www.shmoop.com/quotes/fairy-tales-are-more-than-true.html (archived at https://perma.cc/77M2-KGTV)

40 Cotton, B (2019) Meet Ayesha Ofori: the property entrepreneur out to raise up neglected communities, *Business Leader*, 18 July, https://www.businessleader. co.uk/meet-ayesha-ofori-the-property-entrepreneur-out-to-raise-up-neglected-communities/70934/ (archived at https://perma.cc/837B-9XLU)

Chapter 7

1 Chamorro-Premuzic, T (2019) *Why Do So Many Incompetent Men Become Leaders? (And How to Fix It)*, Harvard Business Review Press, Boston, MA

2 Paul, K (2020) Trump tweets his way to a record on impeachment day, *Business Insider*, 23 January, https://www.theguardian.com/us-news/2020/jan/22/ trump-impeachment-tweet-record (archived at https://perma.cc/4X88-YUYB)

3 Bickart, B, Fournier, S and Nisenholtz, M (2017) What Trump understands about using social media to drive attention, *Harvard Business Review*, 1 March, https://hbr.org/2017/03/what-trump-understands-about-using-social-media-to-drive-attention (archived at https://perma.cc/F9KK-RD2H)

4 HSE (nd) A safe place of work, Health and Safety Executive, https://www.hse. gov.uk/toolbox/workplace/facilities.htm (archived at https://perma.cc/2ERE-G2CU)

5 Hartmans, A (2019) Silicon Valley's ultimate status symbol is the sneaker. Here are the rare, expensive, and goofy shoes worn by the top tech CEOs, *Business Insider*, 15 March, https://www.businessinsider.com/sneakers-worn-by-tech-execs-2017-5?r=US&IR=T (archived at https://perma.cc/V3QX-WXXV)

6 Whitbourne, S K (2016) 4 ways to deal with insecure people: start by managing your own feelings, *Psychology Today*, 27 February, https://www. psychologytoday.com/gb/blog/fulfillment-any-age/201602/4-ways-deal-insecure-people (archived at https://perma.cc/9DGK-LX8S)

7 Neate, R (2019) Hubris of a high flyer: how investors brought WeWork founder down to earth, *Guardian*, 28 September, https://www.theguardian. com/business/2019/sep/28/hubris-of-a-high-flyer-how-investors-brought-wework-founder-down-to-earth (archived at https://perma.cc/7JGX-T5U8)

Chapter 8

1 https://gmat.economist.com/gmat-advice/gmat-overview/gmat-scoring/ how-gmat-scored (archived at https://perma.cc/JZ7L-VR8F)

2 https://www.cdc.gov/healthyyouth/health_and_academics/pdf/ DASHfactsheetSuicidal.pdf (archived at https://perma.cc/K7J7-HWPY)

3 https://leighacademiestrust.org.uk/ (archived at https://perma.cc/L9UW-WERD)

4 Garner, R (2015) Sir Anthony Seldon: historian says test obsession wrecks education, *Independent*, 19 December, https://www.independent.co.uk/news/education/education-news/sir-anthony-seldon-historian-says-test-obsession-wrecks-education-a6779891.html (archived at https://perma.cc/3W86-2ER8)

5 Ferrier, M (2012) Gradgrind: my favourite Charles Dickens character, *Telegraph*, 13 February, https://www.telegraph.co.uk/culture/charles-dickens/9048771/Gradgrind-My-favourite-Charles-Dickens-character.html (archived at https://perma.cc/9G9Y-7QK4)

6 George, R P (2019) Education 20/20: Robert P George's concluding statement, *YouTube*, 2 April [video] https://www.youtube.com/watch?v=7UfRLFTFDJ4 (archived at https://perma.cc/6M7M-JYK6)

7 Isaacson, W (2008) *Einstein: His life and universe*, Simon & Schuster, London

8 https://www.famousscientists.org/7-great-examples-of-scientific-discoveries-made-in-dreams/ (archived at https://perma.cc/3ZBD-GLWF)

9 Lewis, C (2016) *Too Fast to Think: How to reclaim your creativity in a hyper-connected work culture*, Kogan Page, London

10 Frangos, C (2018) Making leadership last: how long-tenure CEOs stand their ground, *Forbes*, 3 December, https://www.forbes.com/sites/cassandrafrangos/2018/12/03/making-leadership-last-how-long-tenure-ceos-stand-their-ground/#67949bca132e (archived at https://perma.cc/C8CB-4PV5)

11 Schmidt, E (2018) For the first time, 90 percent completed high school or more, United States Census Bureau, 31 July, https://www.census.gov/library/stories/2018/07/educational-attainment.html (archived at https://perma.cc/CUU8-T76Y)

12 https://www.statista.com/statistics/184272/educational-attainment-of-college-diploma-or-higher-by-gender/ (archived at https://perma.cc/SFM2-Z9UM)

13 Longenecker, D (2016) Benedict means business, *The Imaginative Conservative*, 25 September, https://theimaginativeconservative.org/2016/09/benedict-means-business-longenecker-timeless.html (archived at https://perma.cc/V6F8-9JNK)

14 https://www.goodreads.com/quotes/183226-take-rest-a-field-that-has-rested-gives-a-beautiful (archived at https://perma.cc/3TMJ-DYHD)

15 Interview with the author.

Chapter 9

1 Ball, P (2009) *Universe of Stone: Chartres Cathedral and the triumph of the medieval mind*, Vintage Books, London

2 Cohen, N (2009) Microsoft Encarta dies after long battle with Wikipedia, *New York Times*, 30 March, https://bits.blogs.nytimes.com/2009/03/30/microsoft-encarta-dies-after-long-battle-with-wikipedia/ (archived at https://perma.cc/SF7Y-WQN7)

3 https://corpgov.law.harvard.edu/2018/02/12/ceo-tenure-rates/ (archived at https://perma.cc/6NPS-X925)

Index